P9-DGD-942

TYLER'S ULTIMATE

TYLER'S ULTIMATE

BRILLIANT SIMPLE FOOD TO MAKE ANYTIME

TYLER FLORENCE

PHOTOGRAPHS BY PETRINA TINSLAY

Clarkson Potter/Publishers
New York

COPYRIGHT © 2006 BY TYLER FLORENCE
PHOTOGRAPHS COPYRIGHT © 2006 BY PETRINA TINSLAY

ALL RIGHTS RESERVED.
PUBLISHED IN THE UNITED STATES BY CLARKSON POTTER/PUBLISHERS,
AN IMPRINT OF THE CROWN PUBLISHING GROUP,
A DIVISION OF RANDOM HOUSE, INC., NEW YORK.
WWW.CROWNPUBLISHING.COM
WWW.CLARKSONPOTTER.COM

CLARKSON N. POTTER IS A TRADEMARK AND POTTER AND
COLOPHON ARE REGISTERED TRADEMARKS OF RANDOM HOUSE, INC.

LIBRARY OF CONGRESS CATALOGING-IN-PUBLICATION DATA
IS AVAILABLE UPON REQUEST

ISBN-13: 978-1-4000-5238-7
ISBN-10: 1-4000-5238-6

PRINTED IN THE UNITED STATES OF AMERICA

DESIGN BY RUBA ABU-NIMAH & KEVIN LEY

10 9 8 7 6

FOR MY SON, MILES

CONTENTS

INTRODUCTION

ONCE A YEAR I GET THIS DEEP ITCH TO GO TO EUROPE, SOAK UP THE
CULTURE, COOK, EAT, LIVE, AND DREAM GREAT FOOD. *So last summer I
packed up the family and went off to spend the last two weeks of July in one
of my favorite spots, a small town in the south of France about 30 minutes
north of Nice. It was lavender season. The air was sweet, and I was hungry—hungry to re-charge my batteries, clear my head, immerse myself in
food, and write this book.*

*Twice a week I drove along country roads lined with fields of huge, yellow
sunflowers into Nice, where I strolled through open-air markets and reminded
myself why I love being a chef. Shopping in these markets is a truly amazing
experience: The scent of tomato vines clings to the air as shoppers and mer-
chants baggle over prices, each enacting the rituals inherent to the mysterious
French religion of food. Everywhere you look there is something delicious.
Rounds of un-pasteurized cheeses taste as rich as butter, frozen in time.
Briny oysters covered in perfect, tiny barnacles taste like little sips of seawater. Young chickens, cavities stuffed with fresh herbs, spin slowly on rotis-
series; their skin is crisp and golden and the smell is just incredible.*

*There are crocks of gleaming multihued olives as juicy as grapes, hanging
ropes of smoky saucissons, and aubergines, black as midnight, practically
begging to be stewed into ratatouille. Standing there among the food stalls, I
drank in all of those colors and smells and tastes and I couldn't wait to get
home to cook. I'd leave carrying so many plastic bags that the tips of my
fingers turned purple and I couldn't have been happier.*

*Once back at the house I'd head straight for the kitchen, unpack the bags,
and fire up the stoves. And then I was on my way, transforming what I'd
seen at the market into great, simple home cooking. One night, inspired by
those gorgeous rotisserie birds, I smeared a chicken all over with a rich, green
paste of chopped parsley, thyme, tarragon, garlic, and olive oil, threw the
chicken in a roasting pan with hunks of zucchini, tomato, and onion and
roasted it all until the chicken was infused with the scent of the herbs and the
vegetables melted alongside it.*

*Another day, inspired by the pizza-like onion tarts native to that part of
France, I spread hunks of baguette with caramelized onions, tossed on olives,
thyme, and anchovies for flavor and local color, then showered it all with
grated Parmigiano and threw it in the oven to crisp. The smell brought the*

...AN EXPERIENCE OF THE "ULTIMATE" IN PLEASURE FOR ME —A STATE OF MIND ABOUT FEEDING MYSELF AND MY FRIENDS AND FAMILY WELL AND ENJOYING SIMPLE PLEASURES OVER AN AMAZING MEAL.

kids running in from the pool where they'd been hanging out. We scarfed that down and followed it up with sautéed sausages served with apples caramelized in the pan drippings and a little brown sugar, buttered cabbage, and mashed potatoes. Simple and delicious.

That summer was an experience of the "Ultimate" in pleasure for me—a state of mind about feeding myself and my friends and family well and enjoying simple pleasures over an amazing meal. This book is an expression of all that in recipes—the ultimate in delicious simple home cooking, the ultimate in accessibility, the ultimate in translating food from around the world—from restaurants, from homes, from street food—into a dish you can put together in a reasonable amount of time in your own home with the ultimate confidence that you're going to knock it out of the park.

You don't need to be in the south of France to cook this way. When I got home to New York, I scoured my local grocery stores for my favorite ingredients (and yeah, it helps to live in Chinatown, but supermarkets these days carry an abundance of ethnic foods so it's easier and easier to find great stuff from all over the world). And I kept searching for those amazing, ultimate dishes that anyone can make at home—for a birthday, a backyard barbecue, or just because it's Tuesday night.

Check out the Ultimate Crab Cakes, the best crab cakes I've ever eaten, made with big hunks of jumbo lump crabmeat and fresh breadcrumbs. What you taste is sweet, fresh seafood just barely held together by light breading; they're dynamite with smoky chipotle mayonnaise. The Ultimate Fried Chicken, borrowed from my good friend Cesare Casella at Maremma restaurant in New York City, is just about the best fried chicken you can make because the chicken is perfumed with fresh herbs and garlic. And you don't have to own a restaurant in New York to make it. Or Lemon Curry Chicken, a simple chicken stew inspired by the flavors of India and served with a rice salad spiked with sweet mango, crunchy cashews, and mint; you'll whip it up in under an hour—the quickest trip to India you'll ever take.

I love the craft of cooking, I love traveling, and I love sharing it all with you. As the years go by I will still be here slugging away in the kitchen and finding amazing recipes that we can cook together. It's been a great ride so far and I can't thank you enough for your continued support. I hope that with this book I have created a cooking tool that you will really use. So don't be shy…dig in!

TYLER FLORENCE • NEW YORK CITY

With everyone's lives so crazy, there's something really practical about having delicious, small bites of food on the table for friends and family when they walk in the door. It buys you another half hour in the kitchen while the rest of the meal cooks, and it gives everybody a chance to relax with a glass of wine. Starters, appetizers, or first course, whatever you want to call them, they don't have to be complicated or over the top. Everything works, from something as simple as juicy, roasted cherry tomato salsa served with a big bowl of tortilla chips, to a delicious creamy soup that takes two seconds to buzz down in a blender. Some of these appetizers are substantial enough for a full meal, if it's just two of you. Here's a collection of recipes that will give you a little breathing space and make you look like a superhero at your dinner party.

THE ULTIMATE CHICKEN WINGS WITH CURRY-LIME BUTTER

CURRY-LIME BUTTER TAKES CHICKEN WINGS IN A WHOLE DIFFERENT DIRECTION. *The butter is sweet from a couple of drops of honey and bright with lime zest; Thai red curry paste—you can pick it up at any grocery store—wraps it all up with a really complex heat. I like to serve the wings on a big platter and let people tear through them. Curry-lime butter is also great on a piece of simple grilled fish.*

SERVES 4 TO 6

4 pounds whole chicken wings

Extra-virgin olive oil

Kosher salt and freshly ground black pepper

½ cup (1 stick) unsalted butter, softened

2 teaspoons Thai red curry paste

Zest and juice of 1 lime

1 tablespoon honey

Splash of soy sauce

Handful of cilantro leaves, for garnish

Preheat the oven to 425°F.

Rinse the wings under cool water and pat dry. Put the wings in a bowl, drizzle with olive oil, season well with salt and pepper, then toss to coat. Spread the wings out on a baking sheet and roast for 25 to 30 minutes, until the skin gets crisp and brown and the meat is tender.

While you wait, throw the butter, red curry paste, lime zest and juice, honey, and soy sauce into a blender. Season with salt and blend to mix. Scrape the curry-lime butter into a big bowl. When the wings come out of the oven slide them right into the bowl with the butter. Give them a toss and you're done. Scatter the cilantro leaves on top and serve.

CARAMELIZED ONION TOAST

I GO TO THE SOUTH OF FRANCE FOR A FEW WEEKS EVERY SUMMER. *The boulangerie, or bakery, in town sells the most amazing savory pastry called a* pissaladière, *something like a thin focaccia topped with heaps of caramelized onions and dotted with salty anchovies and Niçoise olives. I figured out how to pull off the same effect at home by topping toasted slices of an everyday baguette with a layer of onions caramelized until golden and finishing it off with shaved Parmigiano. The anchovies and olives are optional, but trust me, the flavors they add are amazing.*

SERVES 6 TO 8

4 tablespoons (½ stick) unsalted butter, plus 4 tablespoons (½ stick), softened, for brushing the bread

2 onions, sliced

12 anchovy fillets, chopped (optional)

2 teaspoons fresh thyme leaves

Kosher salt and freshly ground black pepper

1 baguette

⅓ cup pitted Niçoise olives (optional)

Extra-virgin olive oil

Chunk of Parmigiano-Reggiano cheese

Preheat the oven to 450°F.

Heat 4 tablespoons of the butter in a large skillet over medium heat. Add the onions, chopped anchovies (if using), thyme, salt, and pepper and cook, stirring occasionally, until the onions are sweet and golden brown, about 20 minutes.

Meanwhile, holding a serrated knife parallel to the cutting board, shave off the rounded top and bottom of the baguette so that it lies flat. Then halve the baguette horizontally to make 2 long slices of bread. Brush both sides of each slice with the softened butter. Put the bread slices on a baking sheet and spread with the onions. Dot with the olives (if using) and drizzle with olive oil. Throw the sheet in the oven and bake until the bread is crispy, about 15 minutes. Use a vegetable peeler to shower the toasts with Parmigiano shavings. Cut into pieces and serve hot.

SHRIMP BISQUE

EVERY TIME I MAKE THIS SOUP I CAN'T GET OVER HOW DELICIOUS IT IS. *The intense flavor comes from shrimp shells, simmered with leeks and orange, and the cream gives it a silky texture. This is a classic soup; I'm definitely putting it on the menu at my next restaurant.*

SERVES 4 TO 6

1½ pounds medium shrimp, in the shell

1 orange

3 tablespoons extra-virgin olive oil

3 tablespoons unsalted butter

2 leeks, trimmed, halved lengthwise, and rinsed well

1 onion, trimmed, peeled, and halved

2 celery stalks, cut into big chunks

2 carrots, peeled and cut into big chunks

3 fresh thyme sprigs

1 bay leaf

2 tablespoons tomato paste

½ teaspoon cayenne

¼ cup brandy

3 tablespoons all-purpose flour

4 cups heavy cream

Kosher salt and freshly ground black pepper

Finely chopped fresh chives, for garnish

Peel and devein the shrimp, reserving the shells; stick the shrimp into the fridge until it's time to eat. Use a vegetable peeler to strip off a couple pieces of orange zest and grate the remaining zest. Cover and refrigerate the grated zest for garnish.

Heat the olive oil in a large pot over medium heat and melt the butter into it. Add the shrimp shells, leeks, onion, celery, carrots, thyme, bay leaf, strips of orange zest, tomato paste, and cayenne. Cook, stirring every now and then, until the shells are red and the vegetables begin to soften, about 10 minutes.

Take the pot off the heat and carefully pour in the brandy. Return the pot to medium heat, cook for a minute more, then sprinkle in the flour, give it a stir, and cook for another 2 minutes. Now add water to cover, 2 to 3 cups, and deglaze, scraping up all the browned bits on the bottom of the pot with a wooden spoon. Add the cream and bring to a boil. Immediately turn the heat down to low and simmer gently until the soup is reduced and thickened, 30 to 45 minutes. Strain into a clean pot and season with salt and pepper.

When you're ready to serve, return the bisque to a simmer, add the shrimp, and cook for 2 to 3 minutes, just to cook the shrimp through. Give the bisque a final taste for seasoning, pour it into warmed soup bowls, and serve garnished with the reserved orange zest and the chives.

THE ULTIMATE
SPICY CRAB SALAD

THIS SALAD LETS THE TWO MAIN INGREDIENTS, CRAB AND AVOCADO, SHINE. *The crab salad, seasoned with a chile mayonnaise, has a slightly spicy bite, but it cools off quickly once you taste the fresh mint. Spread the crab mixture on toasted slices of baguette, toss with cold pasta, or serve as an accompaniment to the roasted beef tenderloin on page 86.*

SERVES 4

1 pint lump crabmeat, picked over for bits of shell and cartilage

¼ cup mayonnaise

1 tablespoon hot chile paste, such as sambal

2 tablespoons chopped fresh cilantro

Juice of ½ lime

Kosher salt and freshly ground black pepper

2 ripe avocados, unpeeled, halved and seeded

4 fresh mint sprigs

Lemon wedges, for garnish

In a medium bowl, stir the crabmeat together with the mayonnaise, chile paste, cilantro, and lime juice, and season with salt and pepper. Stuff each avocado half with a big spoonful of the crab salad. Garnish the plates with mint and lemon wedges.

Variation: The spicy mayonnaise would be equally good with any firm, mild seafood, like shrimp, grilled tuna, or other fish. Serve a spoonful on a cracker or thick potato chip for a cocktail nibble or on a bed of lettuce for an entrée salad.

SPICY TUNA ROLLS WITH SESAME CUCUMBERS

HERE'S A GREAT WAY TO HAVE THE SUSHI EXPERIENCE WITH-OUT HAVING TO GO THROUGH THE TROUBLE OF MAKING RICE. *Sushi-grade tuna makes a big difference in this recipe, so make the extra effort to track it down. A small block of really good tuna goes a long way. Use a sharp knife to cut it into one-quarter- to one-half-inch cubes—the smallest cubes you can manage easily.*

SERVES 4

SESAME CUCUMBERS

1 hothouse cucumber, peeled and sliced

2 tablespoons toasted sesame oil

1½ teaspoons sesame seeds, toasted over low heat in a dry skillet until fragrant

2 tablespoons fresh lemon juice

1 teaspoon kosher salt

½ teaspoon crushed red pepper flakes

SPICY TUNA ROLLS

½ pound sushi-grade tuna

3 tablespoons mayonnaise

1 teaspoon hot chile paste, such as sambal

2 teaspoons sesame seeds, toasted over low heat in a dry skillet until fragrant

¼ teaspoon toasted sesame oil

2 teaspoons fresh lemon juice

2 sheets nori

Radish sprouts, for garnish

First make the cucumber salad. Toss together the cucumber slices, sesame oil, sesame seeds, lemon juice, salt, and red pepper flakes in a bowl. Set it aside so that the cucumber has time to absorb the flavors of the marinade.

Cube the tuna and put it into a medium bowl. Add the mayonnaise, chile paste, sesame seeds, sesame oil, and lemon juice and gently fold that all together.

To assemble the rolls, cut each nori sheet into 4 squares. Put one square on your cutting board but turn it so that it looks like a diamond, with the points at top and bottom. Put a spoonful of tuna in the center and spread it out so that it covers the middle third of the diamond, running from the top to the bottom points. Top with a few radish sprouts. Fold the left side over and then the right, like you're folding a burrito, and seal the nori with a dab of water. Repeat to make 8 tuna rolls. Serve immediately with the sesame cucumbers and garnish with the sprouts.

SALMON CARPACCIO WITH HEARTS OF PALM SALAD AND COCONUT DRESSING

POUNDING SALMON BETWEEN SHEETS OF PLASTIC WRAP GIVES IT THE PAPER-THIN EFFECT OF CARPACCIO. *The thin sheets are so light and delicate, they practically melt in your mouth. The salmon doesn't compete with the other flavors in the dish, so with every bite you get a different sensation.*

SERVES 4 TO 6

MARINATED HEARTS OF PALM

¼ cup rice wine vinegar

1 teaspoon sugar

1 fresh green chile, cut in half lengthwise

1-inch piece of fresh ginger, peeled and smashed with the side of a large knife

1 can (14 ounces) hearts of palm, drained and cut into ¼-inch rings

COCONUT DRESSING

2 firmly packed cups stemmed spinach leaves

1 can (14 ounces) coconut milk

Juice of 1 lime

1 tablespoon fish sauce (nam pla)

Leaves from ½ bunch of fresh cilantro

Kosher salt and freshly ground black pepper

1 pound salmon fillet, skinned and cut into 4 pieces

Radish sprouts, optional

Lime wedges, for serving

In a medium bowl, stir together the vinegar and sugar. Add the chile, ginger, and hearts of palm and give it all a toss. Set that aside while you make the coconut dressing.

Toss the spinach into a blender along with the coconut milk, lime juice, fish sauce, and cilantro and purée until smooth. Season with salt and pepper.

Lay a sheet of plastic wrap on your cutting board and put a piece of salmon in the center. Cover with a second sheet of plastic wrap. Use the flat side of a meat cleaver or a rolling pin to pound the salmon out to a paper-thin sheet. Repeat with the rest of the salmon pieces.

To serve, carefully remove the top sheet of plastic from one of the pieces of salmon. Invert the salmon onto a plate so that the plastic is on top; carefully pull off the plastic. Drizzle with the dressing and scatter some of the hearts of palm salad and a few radish sprouts on top. Make 3 more plates just like this and serve with lime wedges.

WATERMELON GAZPACHO WITH CHILE AND FETA CHEESE

THIS IS TRULY BRILLIANT, SIMPLE COOKING AT ITS FINEST BECAUSE THE RECIPE HAPPENS ALMOST ENTIRELY IN A BLENDER. *I first tasted watermelon and tomato together two summers ago at a restaurant in France in a bright, fresh salad that really captured the essence of summer. For a twist, I took those two flavors and turned them into a gazpacho in which the sugar in the watermelon balances out the bright acidity of the tomatoes.*

SERVES 4 TO 6

3 cups coarsely chopped fresh tomatoes (about 6 large tomatoes)

3 cups cubed and seeded fresh watermelon (about 8 ounces)

1 serrano chile

2 tablespoons red wine vinegar

¼ cup extra-virgin olive oil

2 tablespoons minced red onion

1 cucumber, peeled, seeded, and minced

2 tablespoons minced fresh dill, plus more sprigs for garnish

Kosher salt and freshly ground black pepper

¼ cup crumbled feta cheese

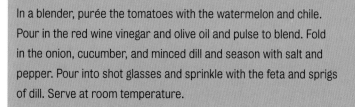

In a blender, purée the tomatoes with the watermelon and chile. Pour in the red wine vinegar and olive oil and pulse to blend. Fold in the onion, cucumber, and minced dill and season with salt and pepper. Pour into shot glasses and sprinkle with the feta and sprigs of dill. Serve at room temperature.

THE ULTIMATE ANTIPASTO PLATTER

NO APPETIZER SECTION WOULD BE COMPLETE WITHOUT A STUDY OF THE ITALIAN TRADITION OF ANTIPASTO, *which, literally translated, means "before the pasta." An antipasto platter is an array of small bites of food generally consisting of briny olives, salty cured meats, sharp cheeses, and roasted marinated vegetables, all to be consumed with crunchy chunks of bread. It's also a quick and elegant way to get a dinner party started while you finish up the main course in the kitchen.*

Here through page 39 you'll find a hit list of simple, rustic recipes that I've picked up over the past few years. Very few of them actually require any actual cooking. Most are as simple as buying really good Serrano ham and wrapping it around some sweet slices of cantaloupe, or soaking deli olives in a marinade of olive oil, orange, rosemary, and crushed red pepper.

BOCCONCINI TIED WITH PROSCIUTTO

THIS IS A GREAT STARTER *that I like to put together for cocktail parties. It's as simple as stopping by a deli counter and grabbing ¼ pound of thinly sliced prosciutto and a few of the small, creamy balls of fresh mozzarella called bocconcini. Bocca means mouth in Italian, and when I serve this appetizer the smiles show me that everybody loves them. It doesn't matter what time of the year it is, one little bite tastes like the ultimate poolside snack filled with deep Mediterranean flavors.*

MAKES 6
CHILE OIL
2 cups extra-virgin olive oil

4 fresh thyme sprigs

4 fresh rosemary sprigs

1½ tablespoons dried red chili flakes

2 strips of orange peel

BOCCONCINI
6 bocconcini (small mozzarella balls)

6 strips of prosciutto

Fresh rosemary and thyme sprigs, for garnish

Combine the oil, thyme, rosemary, chili flakes, and orange peel in a small bowl or jar. Set aside and let it sit for at least one hour to allow the flavors to infuse.

Wrap each bocconcini in a strip of prosciutto and use a toothpick to secure. Drizzle the bocconcini with the infused chile oil and garnish with fresh rosemary and thyme.

HERBED GOAT CHEESE BITES

PRESSING BAGUETTE SLICES INTO THE BOTTOM *of a muffin tin before you toast them creates a spoon shape when they come out of the oven and they're super crisp. The goat cheese gets rolled in chopped fresh herbs and sliced into circles, and if the cheese is cold from the fridge and your knife is wet, the slices come out perfect.*

MAKES 16 TO 20

1 tablespoon fresh thyme leaves

1 tablespoon fresh flat-leaf parsley

1 tablespoon fresh tarragon

1 tablespoon fresh mint

1 8-ounce log soft fresh goat cheese

1 baguette

2 tablespoons extra-virgin olive oil

½ cup oil-packed sun-dried tomatoes

½ cup fresh basil leaves

Combine the thyme, parsley, tarragon, and mint leaves on a cutting board and chop them finely together. Unwrap the log of goat cheese and roll it in the chopped herbs, pressing the herbs to adhere.

Preheat the oven to 350°F.

Cut the baguette into thin slices and drizzle them with a little extra-virgin olive oil. Gently press slices into a muffin tray so that they form a boat-like shape and bake for 5 to 7 minutes. They should be lightly browned and crisp. Let the baguette slices cool in the muffin tin.

Top each baguette slice with a slice of herbed goat cheese. Top with a sun-dried tomato and garnish with fresh basil leaves.

SPANISH HAM AND MELON WITH SPICED VINAIGRETTE

SPAIN PRODUCES THE FINEST HAM IN THE WORLD. *The rich flavor of their ham is salty and dense. It's not as buttery as prosciutto but the flavor is better. Wrapped around sweet chunks of cold melon, it's a flavor match made in heaven.*

SERVES 12 TO 16

SHERRY WINE VINAIGRETTE

¼ cup sherry wine vinegar

1 tablespoon honey

1 shallot, sliced thinly

½ teaspoon ground fenugreek

½ tespoon fresh thyme leaves

½ cup of olive oil

1 cantaloupe

½ pound Serrano ham

Combine the vinegar, honey, shallots, ground fenugreek, and thyme in a large bowl. Slowly whisk in the olive oil.

Slice the melon into thin wedges and cut ¾ of the way between the skin and flesh. Top the wedges of melon with slices of Serrano ham and drizzle with the vinaigrette.

MANCHEGO QUINCE SKEWERS

MANCHEGO IS THE KING OF SPANISH CHEESES. *Similar to Italian provolone in flavor, this slightly salty cheese is the anchor for a delicious hors d'oeuvre. Quince paste, which is available in most cheese shops, gets rolled in toasted chopped almonds. Elegant and cool, these classic flavors fly off the plate.*

MAKES ABOUT 20

1 pound quince paste (see note)

1 cup almonds

1 pound Manchego cheese (see note)

1 bunch watercress

Preheat the oven to 350°F.

Spread the almonds on a baking sheet and toast until lightly browned, about 10 minutes. Cool, then transfer to a food processor and pulse until finely chopped.

Cut the quince paste into 1-inch cubes and roll them in the chopped almonds. Cut the cheese into 1-inch cubes.

Thread each quince cube onto a toothpick, then a watercress leaf followed by a cube of cheese.

Note: Parmigiano-Reggiano can be substituted for the Manchego. Quince paste can be found in cheese shops or Latin markets.

FIGS WITH GOAT CHEESE AND HONEY

_____

SERVES 10 TO 12

1 pint fresh black figs

½ pound fresh, soft goat cheese

Cracked black pepper

2 tablespoons honey

½ bunch arugula leaves

Rinse the figs and cut in half lengthwise. Roll the goat cheese into small balls and sprinkle them with fresh cracked black pepper. Arrange the figs and goat cheese on a plate. Drizzle the figs with honey and garnish with the arugula.

ROASTED PEPPER SALAD

_____

SERVES 6 TO 8

3 large red peppers

2 tablespoons balsamic vinegar

2 tablespoons extra-virgin olive oil

Kosher salt

Fresh ground black pepper

2 fresh oregano sprigs

Roast the peppers directly over a gas burner or in a 400°F oven until blistered; cover with plastic wrap and steam for 15 minutes, then peel, core, and cut into fat slices.

Season the peppers with balsamic vinegar, extra-virgin olive oil, and salt and pepper. Garnish with the fresh oregano.

ROASTED EGGPLANT WITH LEMON AND PARSLEY

_____

SERVES 12 TO 16

3 garlic cloves, minced

2 tablespoons chopped flat-leaf parsley

Grated zest of ½ lemon

1 cup extra-virgin olive oil

Pinch of sugar

Pinch of salt

Fresh ground black pepper

2 medium eggplants, sliced ¼-inch thick

⅓ cup red wine vinegar

Preheat the oven to 400°F.

Combine the garlic, parsley, lemon zest, ½ cup of the olive oil, sugar, and salt and pepper to make a paste. Toss with the eggplant slices to coat. Arrange the eggplant slices on a baking sheet in a single layer and roast until super soft. Baste occasionally with the remaining oil.

Arrange the roasted slices on a platter in a single layer and drizzle with the vinegar.

MARINATED CHICKPEAS

SERVES 6 TO 8

1 garlic clove, peeled and smashed

1 fresh red chile, thinly sliced

1 tablespoon cumin seeds

1 teaspoon paprika

2 tablespoons extra-virgin olive oil

1 (15.5-ounce) can chickpeas, drained

½ teaspoon kosher salt

Juice of ½ lemon

Sauté the garlic, chile, cumin, and paprika in olive oil until fragrant, a minute or two. Let cool and pour over the chickpeas; season with salt and lemon juice. Puree about ⅓ of the chickpeas in a food processor until creamy, then combine with the whole chickpeas.

OLIVES WITH ROSEMARY AND ORANGE

MAKES 2 CUPS

1 pound mixed olives, black and green

2 garlic cloves, peeled and crushed

2 rosemary sprigs

2 orange slices

2 hot chiles

2 cups extra-virgin olive oil

Place the olives in a jar that just fits them without packing tightly. Combine the garlic, rosemary, orange slices, chiles, and olive oil in a saucepan and bring slowly to a simmer to infuse the oil and soften the garlic.

Pout the oil over the olives and let cool. Serve at room temperature.

SERVES 10 TO 12

10 baby artichokes

2 tablespoons extra-virgin olive oil

2 garlic cloves, peeled and smashed

DRESSING

2 tablespoons extra-virgin olive oil

2 anchovy fillets

2 tablespoons chopped fresh mint

Kosher salt and fresh ground black pepper

2 lemons, cut into wedges

Preheat the oven to 400°F.

Trim the stems of the artichokes and cut off the prickly leaf tips. Pull off the tough outer leaves until only pale tender leaves remain. Heat the oil in a skillet with the garlic, then brown the artichokes for a few minutes. Roast in the oven until tender, about 25 minutes. Combine the dressing ingredients in a blender and pour over the roasted artichokes. Serve with lemon wedges.

ROASTED CAULIFLOWER SOUP

CAULIFLOWER GETS A BAD RAP. *In my opinion it's the unsung hero of the vegetable world. The origin of this recipe is a humble side dish my parents used to make when I was a kid, simply cauliflower steamed to within an inch of its life, with butter and salt. On a cool autumn night, nothing tasted better. I took those classic flavors and translated them into a soup that presents deep, rustic sweet cabbage flavor with a really silky texture. This recipe should get the underappreciated cauliflower onto the A-list at long last.*

_____

SERVES 4 TO 6

SOUP

1 quart milk

Kosher salt

1 head of cauliflower, cored and broken into florets

½ onion, sliced

8 fresh thyme sprigs

½ cup (1 stick) unsalted butter

1 bay leaf

Extra-virgin olive oil

Freshly ground black pepper

BRIOCHE–CAULIFLOWER CRUMBS

4 slices brioche, toasted

¼ cup pine nuts

4 tablespoons (½ stick) unsalted butter, melted

2 tablespoons chopped fresh flat-leaf parsley

Pour the milk into a large saucepan, add a little salt, and bring to a simmer over medium heat. Set aside about ½ cup cauliflower florets for garnish and put the rest of the cauliflower in the pan with the milk. Add the onion, 4 thyme sprigs, the butter, and the bay leaf. Bring to a simmer, cover, and cook for 12 to 15 minutes, until the cauliflower is tender. Discard the thyme and bay leaf, then purée the soup in a blender. Pour the soup back into the saucepan and season with a drizzle of olive oil, salt, and a little pepper. (White pepper is very cool here if you have it; if not, use black pepper sparingly.)

While that's cooking, preheat the oven to 350°F. Grate the toasted brioche slices on a box grater. Thinly slice the reserved cauliflower florets and combine with the brioche crumbs, the leaves from the remaining 4 thyme sprigs, and pine nuts in a bowl. Drizzle with the melted butter and toss. Spread the mixture on a baking sheet and toast in the oven until lightly browned and crispy, 5 to 7 minutes. Remove from the oven, scrape into a bowl, and stir in the parsley.

To serve, pour the soup into serving bowls and drizzle with a little more olive oil. Sprinkle with the brioche-cauliflower crumbs.

MUSSELS WITH WHITE WINE AND THYME

LIKE THE OLD OYSTER ROASTS THAT I GREW UP WITH ON THE COAST OF SOUTH CAROLINA, THIS DISH SHOULD BE SERVED IN THE POT *on a picnic table covered with newspaper. Everyone stands over the table tearing into the mussels, getting garlic butter all over their fingers as they dip chunks of bread into the sweet briny liquid at the bottom of the pot. Wash the whole thing down with a couple of cold beers and you've got a night you'll be talking about for weeks.*

SERVES 4

4 pounds mussels

4 tablespoons (½ stick) unsalted butter

2 tablespoons extra-virgin olive oil

2 garlic cloves, peeled and smashed

4 fresh thyme sprigs

½ lemon, thinly sliced

¾ cup dry white wine

½ cup low-sodium chicken broth

Kosher salt and freshly ground black pepper

Herbed Garlic Bread (recipe follows)

Scrub the mussels with a vegetable brush under cold running water; discard any with broken shells or that remain opened when tapped. In a large pot over medium heat, melt the butter in the olive oil. Add the garlic, thyme, and lemon slices and cook until everything has softened, about 5 minutes. Add the mussels and stir to coat them with all the flavors. Add the wine, then the chicken broth; bring to a boil, then reduce the heat to a simmer, cover the pot, and cook for 10 to 12 minutes, until the mussels open. (Discard any mussels that remain closed.) Taste the sauce for salt and pepper. Bring the pot to the table and divide the mussels and sauce among serving bowls. Serve with plenty of garlic bread.

HERBED GARLIC BREAD (MAKES 1 LOAF)

½ cup (1 stick) unsalted butter, softened

2 garlic cloves, mashed to a paste

2 tablespoons chopped fresh flat-leaf parsley

2 tablespoons chopped fresh basil

Kosher salt and freshly ground black pepper

1 crusty baguette

Preheat the oven to 400°F. Stir together the butter, garlic, and herbs in a small bowl and season with salt and pepper. Tear the loaf of bread open lengthwise and spread the herb-garlic mixture over both halves. Close it up again, wrap in aluminum foil, and bake for 15 minutes.

CHICKEN LIVER PÂTÉ

MY SON AND I WERE TALKING ABOUT MUSIC ONE DAY *and I mentioned a Led Zeppelin album. He said, "Daddy, what's an album?" That's the way I feel about chicken liver pâté: It's a delicious, soulful anachronism. You know what? I'm bringing it back. It's cool. With crusty bread and sweet fresh grapes, it's a whole lot of love; and it's really easy to make.*

SERVES 8

1 pound chicken livers, trimmed of any membranes or fat

6 tablespoons Port wine

14 tablespoons (1¾ sticks) unsalted butter

2 shallots, chopped

1 garlic clove, crushed

1 teaspoon chopped fresh thyme leaves, plus 1 nice-looking sprig for garnish

¼ cup heavy cream

Kosher salt and freshly ground black pepper

1 brioche loaf or baguette, sliced

Halved red grapes, for serving

Rinse the livers and pat them dry. Put them in a small bowl, pour the Port over them, cover, and refrigerate for 2 hours.

Melt 3 tablespoons of the butter in a medium skillet. Add the shallots, garlic, and chopped thyme and cook over medium-low heat, stirring often, until softened but not brown, 3 to 4 minutes. Add the livers, reserving the Port, and cook without browning until the livers just change color, 3 to 4 minutes. (Browning would toughen the exterior of the livers so the pâté would not be smooth.) Add the reserved Port and simmer for 2 minutes. Put all that in a blender and purée until smooth. Add 3 more tablespoons of butter and process again until smooth. Now pour in the cream and pulse just until incorporated. Season with salt and pepper.

Spoon the mixture into a 3-cup terrine or loaf pan (or into Mason jars) and smooth the surface. Refrigerate for 1 hour, or until the pâté just firms up. Then melt the remaining 8 tablespoons of butter and pour it over the top of the pâté to cover completely (this will seal the pâté and keep it from discoloring). Press the thyme sprig into the butter and refrigerate overnight until the pâté is completely firm or up to a week.

When you're ready to serve, toast the bread slices at 350°F on a baking sheet until lightly browned and crisp, 5 to 7 minutes. Serve the pâté with the toasts and red grape halves.

THE ULTIMATE FRENCH ONION SOUP

THE FRENCH ARE FAMOUS FOR WHAT I CALL THE HIGH ART OF "PEASANT FOOD," *in this case, the transformation of a humble onion into a rich bouillon flavored with herbs and red wine—truly one of the most satisfying things I've ever tasted. A bowl of onion soup topped with a French-bread crouton and melted Gruyère cheese makes an elegant cold-weather starter, but if nobody else is around, it's a perfect TV dinner, too.*

SERVES 4 TO 6

½ cup (1 stick) unsalted butter, plus 4 tablespoons (½ stick), softened

4 onions, sliced

2 garlic cloves, chopped

1 bay leaf

2 fresh thyme sprigs

Kosher salt and freshly ground black pepper

1 cup red wine

3 tablespoons all-purpose flour

2 quarts beef broth

1 baguette, sliced

½ pound grated Gruyère cheese

Chopped fresh chives, for garnish

Melt the stick of butter in a large pot over medium heat. Add the onions, garlic, bay leaf, thyme, and salt and pepper and cook until the onions are very soft and caramelized, about 25 minutes. Add the wine, bring to a boil, reduce the heat, and simmer until the wine has evaporated and the onions are dry, about 5 minutes. Discard the bay leaf and thyme sprigs. Dust the onions with the flour and give them a stir. Turn the heat down to medium-low so the flour doesn't burn, and cook for 10 minutes to cook out the raw flour taste. Now add the beef broth, bring the soup back to a simmer, and cook for 10 minutes. Season to taste with salt and pepper.

When you're ready to eat, preheat the broiler. Arrange the baguette slices on a baking sheet in a single layer and brush with the softened butter. Sprinkle the slices with the Gruyère and broil until bubbly and golden brown, 3 to 5 minutes.

Ladle the soup into bowls and float some of the Gruyère croutons on top. Garnish with chives.

ROASTED CHERRY TOMATO SALSA

I CAME UP WITH THIS VARIATION ON A CLASSIC SALSA LAST
SUMMER *when I had some cooked cherry tomatoes left over
from another dish. I blended in lime, cilantro, and chiles and
the flavors really surprised me; using cooked tomatoes took
the idea of salsa to a whole new level. Broiling the tomatoes
concentrates their sugars, and olive oil gives the salsa a
creamy texture that's great on a piece of fish and clings to
tortilla chips for dear life.*

SERVES 6 TO 8

2 pints cherry or grape tomatoes

Extra-virgin olive oil

Kosher salt and freshly ground black pepper

Juice of 1 lime

1 fresh green chile, thinly sliced

Big handful of fresh cilantro leaves, torn into pieces by hand

Tortilla chips (recipe follows)

Preheat the broiler. Spread the tomatoes on a sheet pan and drizzle
with olive oil. Sprinkle with salt and pepper. Broil the tomatoes until
they burst, 3 to 5 minutes. Dump the tomatoes into a bowl. Add the
lime juice, chile, cilantro, and a healthy drink of olive oil. Taste for
seasoning. Serve at room temperature, with the chips.

HOMEMADE TORTILLA CHIPS

Vegetable oil for shallow frying

8 to 10 corn tortillas

Kosher salt

Heat 1/2 inch of oil in a heavy skillet or shallow pot until nearly smoking. While the oil heats, cut the tortillas into 6 to 8 wedges each.

Fry the tortilla chips a few at a time until crisp and golden.
Transfer to a paper towel–lined plate to drain and sprinkle with salt
while still hot. Repeat with the remaining tortilla wedges. Serve
warm.

When I'm out shopping or at the grocery store planning dinner, I gravitate first toward the fish counter to see what's available. The glistening fillets spread over the top of the shaved ice smell like fresh cucumber and green seawater. Ruby tuna, wild salmon, fat scallops, pink swordfish—a million possibilities start running through my head. Then I look at my watch and snap out of it when I realize I've got to get dinner on the table in forty-five minutes. The secret to cooking fish is to let the natural flavors shine through and that means one thing: uncomplicated. Here's a bunch of recipes that'll really take the guessing game out of preparing seafood, everything from shrimp bisque to crab cakes to deep Thai flavors.

COCONUT SHRIMP WITH BASMATI RICE, APRICOTS, AND LIME

IF YOU LOVE THAI FOOD, THIS RECIPE IS A GREAT INTRO-DUCTION TO COOKING WITH THE AMAZING FLAVORS OF THAT CUISINE. *And it illustrates just how easy it is to put together. Big flavor doesn't necessarily have to mean a lot of dirty dishes; this quick and delicious meal happens in two pots.*

_____

SERVES 4

COCONUT SAUCE

2 tablespoons peanut oil

2-inch piece of fresh ginger, unpeeled, smashed with the side of a large knife

2 Thai chiles, chopped

2 lemongrass stalks, white parts only, chopped into small pieces

4 shallots, chopped

1 tablespoon tomato paste

2 tablespoons sugar

1 quart coconut milk

2 kaffir lime leaves, or 1 lime, halved

RICE

1 cup basmati rice

1½ teaspoons kosher salt

½ cup dried apricots, halved

3 scallions, white and green parts, finely chopped

Handful of arugula leaves

1½ pounds medium shrimp, shelled and deveined

1 small can straw mushrooms, drained

4 fresh basil sprigs, preferably Thai basil, for garnish

¼ cup salted roasted peanuts, chopped, for garnish

1 lime, quartered, for garnish

First get the sauce going: Heat the oil in a large pot over medium heat. Add the ginger, chiles, lemongrass, and shallots and cook until the shallots are softened, 3 to 4 minutes. Add the tomato paste, sugar, coconut milk, and lime leaves and give it a stir. Bring to a boil, reduce the heat, and simmer, uncovered, for about 25 minutes, until the sauce is reduced by about one third and thickened.

While that's cooking, jump to the rice. Combine the rice, salt, and 2 cups of water in a small saucepan. Bring to a simmer, reduce the heat, cover, and cook until the water is absorbed, about 15 minutes. Stir in the apricots, scallions, and arugula.

To finish, add the shrimp to the pot with the sauce and simmer gently just to cook through, 3 to 4 minutes. Add the straw mush-rooms and stir. Spoon the rice into the bottom of 4 bowls. Spoon the shrimp over along with the sauce and garnish each bowl with basil, peanuts, and a wedge of lime.

PEPPERED SALMON WITH CREAMY CHICKPEA DRESSING AND FRESH GREENS

LEMON-CHICKPEA VINAIGRETTE IS AN EASY-TO-MAKE COMPONENT *that brings a lot of flavor to the dish while balancing the subtle richness of fresh salmon. Add a bag of fresh spinach and you've got a fast, healthy meal you can make in well under an hour.*

SERVES 4

¼ cup black peppercorns

¼ cup coriander seeds

1 pound salmon fillet, skin on

Extra-virgin olive oil

Kosher salt

VINAIGRETTE

1 can (15 ounces) chickpeas

¼ cup extra-virgin olive oil

2 teaspoons ground cumin

1 teaspoon sweet paprika

Juice of 1 lemon

Kosher salt and freshly ground black pepper

1 bag (10 ounces) baby spinach

½ bunch of fresh mint

½ bunch of fresh dill

Lemon wedges, for serving

Put the peppercorns and coriander in a clean spice grinder and pulse to a coarse grind. Pour the mixture out onto a large plate. Roll the salmon in the spices until coated all over.

Heat a 2-count of olive oil in a large skillet over medium-high heat until the oil is smoking. Sprinkle the salmon with salt, add it to the pan, and sear for 4 to 5 minutes to develop a good crust. Turn the fillet and cook for 4 to 5 more minutes on the other side, until the salmon begins to flake apart when gently prodded with a fork. Put the salmon on a plate, cover with foil, and set aside at room temperature.

For the vinaigrette, open the can of chickpeas and dump it straight into a bowl, without draining. Add the olive oil, cumin, paprika, lemon juice, and a little salt and pepper and stir that up. Spoon about half of the vinaigrette into a blender and purée; stir the purée back into the rest of the vinaigrette to thicken.

Toss the spinach, mint, and dill in a large bowl.

To serve, spoon the chickpea vinaigrette into the center of a platter. Set the salmon fillet on top and mound the spinach to one side. Serve with lemon wedges.

THE ULTIMATE CRAB CAKES

THE SECRET TO THE ULTIMATE CRAB CAKE IS TWOFOLD. *First, I use only fresh, jumbo lump crabmeat, which gives the cake a hefty bulk so when you put your fork through it, you pull out pure hunks of delicious crab, not breading. Which brings me to the second point: I use soft, fresh white bread crumbs. Dry bread crumbs soak up all the moisture in the crab and leave the cakes dense, heavy, and dry. Fresh bread crumbs give the mixture just enough structure to make the cakes easy to flip, and they hold in moisture so the cakes are as light as a cloud.*

SERVES 4 TO 6

CRAB CAKES

Extra-virgin olive oil

1 onion, finely minced

2 garlic cloves, finely minced

1 pound jumbo lump crabmeat

1½ cups fresh bread crumbs (made from 3 or 4 slices of white bread with the crusts removed)

2 tablespoons mayonnaise

1 large egg white

Juice of 1 lime

¼ cup chopped fresh cilantro, plus whole leaves, for garnish

Kosher salt and freshly ground black pepper

CHILE MAYONNAISE

1 cup mayonnaise

1 canned chipotle chile in adobo, finely chopped, plus 1 teaspoon of the adobo sauce

Zest and juice of 1 lime

Kosher salt and freshly ground black pepper

Small bunch of mâche or baby greens, for garnish

1 fresh red chile, sliced, for garnish (optional)

1 lime, segments cut free of their membranes, for garnish (optional)

Make the crab cakes first so that they have time to firm up in the fridge before you cook them. Heat a 2-count of olive oil in a frying pan over medium heat. Add the onion and garlic and cook for 5 to 7 minutes, until the onion gets kind of caramelized and delicious. Dump that into a bowl and fold in the crabmeat, bread crumbs, mayonnaise, egg white, lime juice, and cilantro, mixing just until well blended. Season with salt and pepper. Shape the mixture into 6 fat crab cakes. Put them on a plate, cover, and stick them in the refrigerator to chill.

For the chile mayo, put the mayonnaise, chipotle chile, adobo sauce, lime zest and juice, and salt and pepper in a bowl and stir it up. Cover and refrigerate until you're ready to eat.

To serve, heat a 3-count of olive oil in a large sauté pan over medium heat. Add the crab cakes and cook for about 4 minutes on each side, or until they're nice and crisp. Serve with the chile mayonnaise and garnish with the greens and sliced red chile and lime segments, if using.

SCALLOP SALTIMBOCCA

I CAME UP WITH THIS DISH FOR A CHARITY EVENT IN NEW YORK CITY. *I used the traditional method for saltimbocca (which is veal scallopini, sage, and prosciutto), substituting scallops for the veal. The speck (German-style bacon) shrinks like a salty skin around the scallops as they cook, while it seasons the sweet flesh all the way through. The finished scallops are bathed in sage butter and served with caramelized apples. Six hundred people attended that event, and I ran out of scallops in about forty-five minutes. This is terrific with the Velvet Potato Pureé on page 198.*

SERVES 4

12 slices speck or prosciutto

12 large sea scallops

2 tablespoons extra-virgin olive oil

2 tablespoons unsalted butter

12 fresh sage leaves

Kosher salt and freshly ground black pepper

2 Golden Delicious apples, peeled, cored, and cut into wedges

½ lemon

Wrap a strip of speck around the circumference of each scallop and squeeze gently so the speck adheres to the scallops. Tie a length of kitchen string around each scallop to keep the speck in place; trim the ends.

Heat the olive oil and butter in a large skillet over medium-high heat. Add the sage leaves and fry until lightly browned and crisp, 2 to 3 minutes. Gently lift the leaves out of the pan and drain flat on paper towels. Season the scallops with salt and pepper. Add the scallops to the hot pan and cook undisturbed for 2 to 3 minutes on each side, until well browned. Remove the scallops from the pan and put them on a platter. Now add the apples to the pan and give them a quick sauté until wilted and caramelized, 4 to 5 minutes. Season with a squeeze of lemon juice and salt and pepper.

To serve, set 3 scallops on each of 4 plates. Snip off and discard the strings. Spoon the apples around and garnish with sage leaves.

THE ULTIMATE GRILLED SHRIMP

A LOT OF PEOPLE MAKE THE MISTAKE OF PEELING SHRIMP BEFORE THEY THROW THEM ON THE GRILL, *which means a lot of the natural flavor ends up in the garbage can. This is my ultimate go-to shrimp recipe for the summer. You stuff a blend of butter, basil, and lemon juice under the shells of the biggest shrimp you can find. As the shells roast on the grill, the flavor of the shrimp intensifies and the sweet basil butter keeps the meat succulent and juicy. To really bring home the flavors of summer, I like to serve this dish atop a big spoonful of Ratatouille (page 210).*

SERVES 4

1 cup (2 sticks) unsalted butter, softened

Leaves from 1 bunch of fresh basil

2 lemons

Kosher salt and freshly ground black pepper

16 large head-on jumbo shrimp in the shell, shells split down the back

Put a large grill pan on two burners over medium-high heat or preheat an outdoor gas or charcoal grill and get it very hot. If you're using an outdoor grill, take a few paper towels and fold them over several times to make a thick square. Blot a small amount of oil on the paper towel, then carefully and quickly wipe the hot grates of the grill to make a nonstick grilling surface.

Meanwhile, throw the butter into a food processor with the basil leaves (reserve a few for garnish), the juice of one of the lemons, and salt and pepper. Purée. Stuff about half of the butter under the shells of the shrimp (about $\frac{1}{2}$ tablespoon per shrimp). Lay the shrimp on the hot grill and cook for 3 minutes on each side, brushing with the remaining basil butter a few times as they cook.

To serve, put the shrimp on plates and dot with the remaining basil butter. Squeeze the remaining lemon over the shrimp and garnish the plates with basil leaves.

PANCETTA AND TUNA ROAST WITH TUSCAN-STYLE BORLOTTI BEANS AND CHERRY TOMATOES

FRESH TUNA'S DELICATE, CLEAN FLAVOR LENDS ITSELF TO LOTS OF FLAVOR COMBINATIONS. *It's as good with Asian inspirations—ginger and soy—as it is with Mediterranean ingredients such as tomato, black olives, and basil. I've found that the meatiness of fresh tuna even stands up to heartier preparations like this one, in which the tuna loin is wrapped in pancetta, roasted, and presented whole. The spicy taste of the pancetta is amazing with creamy borlotti beans, which you can find on page 196. And cherry tomatoes, broiled with salt, pepper, and olive oil, add a nice, bright pop of flavor.*

SERVES 4

1 pint yellow cherry or grape tomatoes

Extra-virgin olive oil

Kosher salt and freshly ground black pepper

2-pound tuna loin, trimmed, about 4 inches in diameter

16 thin slices pancetta

Borlotti Beans with Woody Herbs (page 196)

Preheat the broiler. On a baking sheet, drizzle the cherry tomatoes with olive oil, sprinkle with salt and pepper, and toss. Put the baking sheet under the broiler and broil until the tomatoes burst, 3 to 5 minutes. Dump the tomatoes into a bowl and season again with a drizzle of oil, salt, and pepper; set the tomatoes aside at room temperature.

Sprinkle the tuna all over with salt and pepper. Lay the tuna on a cutting board and shingle the pancetta slices over it, overlapping slightly, pressing lightly to help the pancetta adhere. Be sure to cover the butt ends as well. Tie in four places with kitchen twine to hold the pancetta in place.

Heat a 3-count of olive oil in a large skillet over medium heat until smoking. Put the tuna in the pan and sear for 5 to 7 minutes, turning for even browning, until the pancetta is nice and crisp but the tuna is still very rare.

To serve, cut the tuna into thick slices. Spoon some beans onto 4 plates and nestle the fish right on top. Garnish with the tomatoes.

GRILLED SWORDFISH WITH LEMON AÏOLI AND ROASTED FENNEL

SWORDFISH CAME OFF THE ENDANGERED SPECIES LIST THIS YEAR AFTER MAKING A REMARKABLE COMEBACK. *Consequently I've started noticing fresh swordfish in the market of a quality I've never seen before; it's scallop sweet and pink. Simply grilled and served with roasted fennel, basil, and a lemon aïoli, this preparation really highlights the fresh, clean flavor of the fish. Start the fennel roasting before you work on the fish so you can toss it on the grill with the fish to give it that great grilled taste.*

SERVES 4

2 fennel bulbs, trimmed and quartered

Extra-virgin olive oil

Kosher salt and freshly ground black pepper

LEMON AÏOLI

Zest and juice of ½ lemon

1 cup mayonnaise

Extra-virgin olive oil

Kosher salt and freshly ground black pepper

4 swordfish steaks, about 1 inch thick (1½ to 2 pounds total)

Handful of fresh basil leaves

Preheat the oven to 400°F. Toss the fennel in a bowl with a drizzle of olive oil and salt and pepper. Dump the fennel onto a baking sheet and roast for about 25 minutes, until soft and caramelized.

Meanwhile, put a large grill pan over two burners and preheat over medium-high heat or preheat an outdoor gas or charcoal grill until very hot. If you're using an outdoor grill, take a few paper towels and fold them over several times to make a thick square. Blot a small amount of oil on the paper towel, then carefully and quickly wipe the hot grates of the grill to make a nonstick grilling surface.

While the grill heats, stir the lemon zest and juice into the mayonnaise. Add a drizzle of olive oil and taste for salt and pepper.

When the grill is hot, rub the swordfish with olive oil and sprinkle with salt and pepper. Lay the fish on the grill and cook for about 4 minutes on each side, until just barely translucent in the center. Add the roasted fennel to the grill and cook a few minutes on each side just to mark it. Put the fish on a platter, scatter the fennel on top, and garnish with the basil. Serve with the lemon aïoli.

ROASTED STRIPED BASS WITH GREEN OLIVE COUSCOUS AND GRAPEFRUIT BUTTER

I LOVE WHOLE FISH THAT'S BEEN EITHER ROASTED OR GRILLED ON THE BONE. *It's amazingly moist and has a whole different flavor than if you just cook the fillets. This dish can be translated for any small whole fish like snapper, sea bass, or trout. The fresh green beans and fennel soak up the grapefruit oil that dresses the couscous—you've got yourself the ultimate side dish for fish. Start the couscous first; you'll need it for stuffing the fish.*

SERVES 4

4 tablespoons (½ stick) unsalted butter

Zest and juice of 1 grapefruit

Extra-virgin olive oil

4 whole striped bass, 1½ pounds each, gutted and scaled

Kosher salt and freshly ground black pepper

Green Olive Couscous (recipe follows)

Grapefruit wedges

Arrange an oven rack about 4 inches from the broiler and preheat the broiler.

Melt the butter in a small saucepan with the grapefruit zest and juice and simmer for a couple minutes to reduce the juice. Oil a large baking sheet. Sprinkle the fish all over with salt and pepper, including inside the cavities. Put the fish in a single layer on the baking sheet, then use your hands or a spoon to stuff the cavities with some of the couscous. Drizzle the fish with some of the grapefruit butter and broil, without turning, until the skin blisters and the fish is cooked through but still translucent at the bone, 12 to 15 minutes. Baste the fish a couple of times with the remaining grapefruit butter as it broils. Serve the fish with the remaining couscous and grapefruit wedges.

GREEN OLIVE COUSCOUS (SERVES 4 TO 6)

One of my favorite products I picked up this year is a California line of flavored olive oils produced by a company in San Raphael called O Olive Oil. They make a great grapefruit olive oil that I use in this recipe. If you can't get hold of it, make your own: Remove the zest from 2 grapefruits in strips with a vegetable peeler, combine with 1 cup extra-virgin olive oil and a pinch of sugar in a blender, and blend until smooth.

Kosher salt

½ pound green beans, trimmed

1½ cups cold water

1 cup couscous

1 tablespoon champagne vinegar or white wine vinegar

2 tablespoons grapefruit olive oil

1 fennel bulb, sliced paper-thin

Freshly ground black pepper

¼ cup pine nuts, toasted

¼ cup halved, pitted green olives

Bring a large pot of salted water to a boil for the beans. Fill a large bowl with ice water and add salt to it until it tastes lightly salty—this is your water bath to refresh the beans. When the water comes to a boil, add the beans and cook until just tender, about 3 minutes. Drain, then refresh in the water bath to keep the bright green color, and drain well again. Cut into ½-inch pieces.

Meanwhile, pour the cold water over the couscous in a medium bowl (using cold water will preserve the grain's nutty crunch). Cover and let stand for about 15 minutes, until all of the water has been soaked up. Combine the vinegar, oil, and fennel in a large bowl, season with salt and pepper, and stir. Fold in the couscous along with the pine nuts, the cooked green beans, olives, and more salt and pepper to taste.

WHITE BEAN AND ROASTED SHRIMP SALAD WITH CHERRY TOMATO VINAIGRETTE

THIS IS AN EASY MAIN-COURSE SALAD TO MAKE ANY NIGHT OF THE WEEK. *The shrimp, bacon, and sage are all roasted on the same sheet pan and the roasted cherry tomatoes, drizzled with olive oil, create their own juicy sauce to dress the beans.*

SERVES 4

1 pound large shrimp, peeled and deveined

4 slices bacon, cut crosswise into ½-inch pieces

Extra-virgin olive oil

Kosher salt

8 fresh sage leaves

Cracked black pepper

1 pint mixed red and yellow cherry or grape tomatoes

1 can (14 ounces) cannellini beans, drained

1 tablespoon red wine vinegar

1 bunch of watercress, stems trimmed just above the rubber band

Preheat the oven to 350°F. Arrange 2 racks in the oven.

Arrange the shrimp in a single layer on half of a large baking sheet and put the bacon pieces on the other half. Drizzle with olive oil, season the shrimp with salt, and scatter the sage leaves and pepper over all. Stick that into the oven and roast for 12 to 15 minutes, or until the shrimp are cooked through and the bacon is crisp and browned and the fat has been rendered.

At the same time, on a second baking sheet, drizzle the tomatoes with olive oil, sprinkle with salt and pepper, and toss. Put the tomatoes in the oven and roast until they burst, about 10 minutes.

Scrape the tomatoes, shrimp, bacon, and any juices into a large bowl. Add the beans, the vinegar, and a healthy drink of olive oil. Season with salt and pepper. Fold in the watercress and you've got dinner.

ANGRY LOBSTER WITH TOMATO-CHILE BUTTER AND FRESH BASIL

"ANGRY LOBSTER" IS A DISH I MASTERED WHEN I WAS A SOUS-CHEF AT A MAFIA JOINT IN TRIBECA. *(I think the dish takes its name from the way the lobster gets whacked.) Old-school Italian guys with pinky rings would come in from Jersey with girls decked out in big hair and gold. A big "angry" lobster on the table, chopped up into succulent chunks, was a status symbol for these guys. I can't really recount my experiences in that restaurant here, but if you ever bump into me on the street, ask me about it.*

SERVES 4

2 live lobsters, 1½ pounds each

½ cup all-purpose flour

Kosher salt and freshly ground black pepper

3 garlic cloves, sliced paper-thin

1 teaspoon crushed red pepper flakes or one fresh red chile

¼ cup extra-virgin olive oil

1 pint cherry tomatoes, halved

2 handfuls of fresh basil leaves

Juice of ½ lemon

4 tablespoons (½ stick) unsalted butter, cut into pieces

First cut the lobsters into pieces. Place a lobster on a cutting board. With a chef's knife, stab the lobster between the eyes and all the way through to the cutting board to kill it quickly. Wrap a towel around the claws and twist them off, then break the knuckles off the claws. Crack the claws with the blunt edge of the knife blade, close to the handle, then sink the knife tip into the crack you've made and twist your wrist—this will break the shell of the claws. Set the knuckles and claws aside. Now insert the tip of the knife into the lobster's back at the opening between the body and the first tail segment and cut off the tail. Cut the tail in half lengthwise, then crosswise into 8 chunks. Cut the body in half lengthwise. Pat the lobster pieces dry with paper towels.

Now season the flour generously with salt and pepper in a large baking dish. Taste the flour—you should taste the seasoning. Combine the garlic, red pepper flakes, and oil in a big skillet. Put the skillet over medium heat and heat slowly until the garlic turns golden to infuse the oil with the flavors of the garlic and red pepper. Roll the lobster bodies and pieces in the flour to give them a little crunch, then toss about half of them into the hot oil. Cook uncovered for 3 to 4 minutes to brown the lobster, then turn and brown the other side, 6 to 8 minutes total. Remove the lobster from the pan and cook the rest the same way. Now put all of the lobster back in the skillet, throw the tomatoes on top, and let that cook for 5 to 6 minutes to soften the tomatoes. Add half of the basil and lemon juice and stir. Toss in the butter and shake the pan to melt the butter and emulsify it into the sauce. Serve the lobster with the sauce, garnished with the remaining basil.

THE ULTIMATE GREEK SALAD WITH GRILLED CALAMARI

BY THIS TIME, CLASSIC GREEK SALAD HAS BECOME MORE AMERICAN THAN GREEK, *but the flavors are pure Mediterranean: olives, oregano, lemon, feta, and tomatoes. If you're a fan of grilled calamari, the dressing makes a sensational marinade; it also works really well with shrimp.*

SERVES 4

10 small whole calamari, bodies only (¾ to 1 pound)

VINAIGRETTE

½ cup extra-virgin olive oil

¼ cup red wine vinegar

4 garlic cloves, chopped

1 tablespoon dried oregano

1 tablespoon fresh oregano leaves, plus extra for garnish

1 tablespoon fresh thyme leaves

Juice of 1 lemon

Kosher salt and freshly ground black pepper

1 pint cherry tomatoes, halved

1 medium red onion, thinly sliced

1 medium cucumber, thinly sliced

½ pound feta cheese, crumbled

½ cup kalamata olives, pitted

1 head of romaine lettuce, torn into bite-size pieces

Lemon wedges, for garnish

Rinse the calamari tubes and pat them dry.

To make the vinaigrette, whisk together the oil, vinegar, garlic, dried and fresh oregano, thyme, and lemon juice, and season with salt and pepper. Pour half of the vinaigrette over the calamari and set the rest aside while you make the salad.

Put a large grill pan on two burners over medium-high heat or preheat an outdoor gas or charcoal grill and get it very hot.

Meanwhile, put the tomatoes, onion, cucumber, cheese, olives, and romaine into a large bowl. Pour the remaining vinaigrette over the salad and toss to combine. Set that aside; the vegetables will marinate while you cook the calamari.

If you're using an outdoor grill, take a few paper towels and fold them over several times to make a thick square. Blot a small amount of oil on the paper towel, then carefully and quickly wipe the hot grates of the grill to make a nonstick grilling surface. Put the calamari on the grill and cook just 2 minutes on each side—no longer or they will be tough. Cut the grilled tubes into rings. To serve, arrange the salad on a large platter and scatter the calamari on top. Garnish with fresh oregano leaves and lemon wedges.

SALT AND PEPPER SALMON WITH SMASHED POTATOES, PEAS, LEMON, PEARL ONIONS, AND MINT

CLOSE YOUR EYES AND IMAGINE THESE FLAVORS ON A PLATE: *crispy seared salmon seasoned liberally with salt and pepper; soft, buttery new potatoes; sweet peas; and crunchy pearl onions, dressed with a healthy drizzle of olive oil and fresh mint. The potato part of this embodies the flavors of spring; it's a spin-off on the classic Irish potato dish colcannon. It's rootsy and simple and soul-satisfying.*

SERVES 4

2 pounds new potatoes

Kosher salt

Extra-virgin olive oil

Freshly ground black pepper

2 boxes (10 ounces each) frozen peas

1 box (10 ounces) frozen pearl onions

3 tablespoons unsalted butter

2 shallots, finely chopped

Grated zest of 1 lemon

¼ cup chopped fresh herbs such as mint, parsley, tarragon, and chives

1 bunch of watercress, stems trimmed just above the rubber band

SALMON

Extra-virgin olive oil

1 salmon fillet (about 2 pounds), skin on, 1½ to 2 inches thick

Kosher salt and freshly ground black pepper

Put the potatoes into a large pot, cover them with cold water, and add a large pinch of salt. Bring to a boil and simmer until the potatoes are fork-tender, 20 to 30 minutes. Drain. Stick a fork into the potatoes, one at a time, lift them out of the colander, and peel with a paring knife. Toss the potatoes into a bowl and crush them roughly. Drizzle with olive oil and season with salt and pepper.

Put the peas and onions in a colander and rinse under cool running water just until thawed. Heat 2 tablespoons olive oil with the butter in a medium saucepan over medium heat until the butter melts. Add the shallots and lemon zest and cook until the shallots are softened but not browned, 2 to 3 minutes. Then add the vegetables, season with salt and pepper, and toss to warm the vegetables. Dump the vegetables over the potatoes in the bowl, sprinkle in the herbs, and taste for salt and pepper. Scatter the watercress over the top then fold it in just until it wilts.

Heat a 2-count of olive oil in a large skillet over medium-high heat until the oil is smoking. Sprinkle the salmon with salt and pepper, add it to the pan, and sear for 4 to 5 minutes to develop a good crust. Then turn and cook 4 to 5 more minutes on the other side until the salmon begins to flake apart when gently prodded with a fork. Transfer the salmon to a platter and serve with the vegetables.

I would be a vegetarian if it weren't for the delicious taste of a juicy steak. In this chapter you'll find recipes and cooking tips that will help take the guesswork out of the meat counter and let you tap into your inner carnivore. Whatever makes your mouth water: from a peppery New York strip with brandied mushrooms, to the perfect slow-cooked pot roast, to slow-roasted ribs that are falling off the bone, to the high art of the ultimate hamburger. If you're a vegetarian, sorry…please skip this chapter and move on to Noodles.

ROASTED TENDERLOIN OF BEEF WITH SPICY CRAB SALAD

THIS IS A RIFF ON A CLASSIC SURF AND TURF. *The turf: thick-cut filet mignon steaks—the easiest cut of meat in the world to cook and just the thing to make everybody happy. There's no waste on these slightly marbleized rounds of beef. They just need a good sear on top of the stove to brown and a gentle roast in the oven to finish them off. A few more minutes in the oven and they're medium-rare; a few more than that and they're well done.*

The surf: a simple spicy crab salad served cold. Summer yellow cherry tomatoes, roasted until their sunny flavor bursts through, holds the thing together. Toss in a few sprigs of fresh arugula and you have an amazing summertime meal.

SERVES 4

Extra-virgin olive oil

4 center-cut beef tenderloin steaks, each about 2 inches thick
   (about 2 pounds total)

Kosher salt and freshly ground black pepper

1 pint yellow cherry or grape tomatoes

The Ultimate Spicy Crab Salad (page 22)

1 bunch of arugula, trimmed

Preheat the oven to 400°F.

Put a medium cast-iron or ovenproof skillet over medium-high heat and get it hot. Drizzle in a 2-count of oil. Sprinkle the beef all over with salt and pepper and sear for about 3 minutes on each side, until well browned. Shove the beef to the side and add the tomatoes to the pan; drizzle with olive oil, sprinkle with salt and pepper, and stir gently to coat. Now put the pan in the oven and roast until the beef is rare and the tomatoes burst, 7 to 8 minutes. (Add 2 more minutes for medium-rare, 5 more minutes for medium.)

To serve, arrange the steaks on a serving plate. Spoon the crab salad over the meat and scatter the tomatoes and arugula on top.

VEAL CHOPS AND ROASTED POTATOES WITH BLUE CHEESE DRESSING AND MINT

THIS RECIPE WAS ORIGINALLY SLATED FOR THICK-CUT PORK CHOPS *but the day we shot the photo, the veal chops at the market looked so beautiful I just had to go with it. The sweet flavor of the caramelized veal really sharpens the taste of the other ingredients. Crispy potatoes and a buttermilk dressing with lots of tart blue cheese wrap themselves around every bite of veal, and the mint finishes the dish with bright flavor.*

Of course, if the pork chops look better than the veal the day you're out shopping, you can go back to the original pork concept. Where you can, you've got to let the ingredients dictate the dish.

SERVES 4

2 pounds small Yukon Gold potatoes, split in half through the
    equator
¼ cup plus 2 tablespoons extra-virgin olive oil
Kosher salt and freshly ground black pepper

DRESSING

½ cup crumbled blue cheese
½ cup buttermilk
2 tablespoons fresh lemon juice
1 bunch of fresh chives, minced

4 thick veal or pork chops, about 3 pounds total
Kosher salt and freshly cracked black pepper
¼ cup extra-virgin olive oil
Leaves from 1 bunch of fresh mint
Lemon wedges, for serving

Preheat the oven to 350°F. In a large mixing bowl, toss the potatoes with ¼ cup of oil and season generously with salt and pepper. Spread the potatoes in a single layer on a baking sheet or in a roasting pan, cut side down, so the cut layer gets super crispy like a French fry. Roast for 30 minutes, or until crispy.

Next, start on the dressing. Put the cheese, buttermilk, and 2 tablespoons of olive oil in a small bowl and stir together with a fork, mashing a little to break up the cheese. Season with the lemon juice, salt, pepper, and chives.

When the potatoes have cooked for 20 minutes, season the veal chops with salt and pepper. Put a large sauté pan over medium-high heat, add the olive oil, and heat until it begins to smoke. Add the veal and sauté until golden brown on the outside and just barely pink inside, 3 to 4 minutes on each side.

To serve, put a chop on each of 4 plates. Put the potatoes into a bowl and drizzle with the dressing. Add the mint and toss. Set one portion of the potatoes on top of each chop. Dust with black pepper and serve with lemon wedges.

THE ULTIMATE BEEF STEW

FOR A PROPER BEEF STEW, THE CUT OF MEAT MAKES ALL THE DIFFERENCE. *The only meat I would ever use is shoulder. Its coarse, chewy texture is perfect for a slow braise and after a couple of hours of gentle cooking, the unctuous meat falls apart on the fork and melts in your mouth.*

But that's just the beginning. As the beef simmers with the red wine, herbs, garlic, and vegetables, it all melds into one decadent flavor. Mix it with a forkful of velvety potato purée, and you have a perfect bite.

———————

SERVES 6

3 pounds beef shoulder, cut into 2-inch cubes

12 fresh thyme sprigs

2 carrots, sliced ¼ inch thick

6 garlic cloves, smashed

2 cups red pearl onions, blanched and peeled

Zest of 1 orange, removed with a zester in large strips

A few whole cloves

1 teaspoon whole black peppercorns

2 bay leaves

1 bottle (750 ml) robust, dry red wine that's good enough that you wouldn't be afraid to drink it

¼ cup extra-virgin olive oil

3 tablespoons unsalted butter

Sea salt and freshly ground black pepper

3½ cups beef broth

4 new potatoes, cut in half

½ pound baby carrots

1 pound white mushrooms, cut in half

Pinch of sugar

½ pound garden peas

Handful of chopped fresh flat-leaf parsley

Handful of chopped fresh chives

Velvet Potato Purée (page 198)

Four hours before you want to start cooking (or the night before), put the beef in a large glass or plastic container. Add 8 of the thyme sprigs, the sliced carrots, garlic, pearl onions, orange zest, cloves, peppercorns, bay leaves, and the wine. Turn that all with your hands to mix, then cover and refrigerate for 4 hours.

When you're ready to cook, take the beef out of the marinade, reserving the marinade, and blot dry on paper towels. Heat the oil and the butter with the remaining 4 thyme sprigs in a heavy-bottomed pot or Dutch oven over high heat. When the oil begins to smoke, discard the thyme sprigs. Add the beef in batches and brown evenly on all sides, 8 to 10 minutes. Return all the beef to the pot and season with salt and pepper. Strain the marinade into the pot with the beef and deglaze, scraping up the browned bits on the bottom of the pot with a wooden spoon. Add the beef broth, bring to a simmer, and cook, uncovered, until the liquid starts to thicken, about 15 to 20 minutes. Then cover, reduce the heat to low, and cook at a slow simmer for 2 hours.

Now uncover the pot and add the potatoes, baby carrots, and mushrooms, along with a pinch of sugar to balance out the acid from the red wine. Turn the heat up slightly and simmer, uncovered, for about 30 minutes more, until the vegetables and meat are tender and the sauce has thickened. Stir in the peas during the final 5 minutes of cooking. Season with salt and pepper. Garnish with chopped parsley and chives and serve with potato purée.

THE ULTIMATE BARBECUED RIBS

IN THE SOUTH, BARBECUE IS CONSIDERED ONE OF THE FIVE
MAJOR FOOD GROUPS, *the others being baked beans, potato
salad, coleslaw, and sweet tea. That deep, rich flavor of pork
ribs falling off the bone is, in my opinion, the definition of
classic American cooking—authentic flavors you can't get
anywhere else.*

SERVES 4 TO 6

2 slabs baby back ribs (about 3 pounds)

THE ULTIMATE BARBECUE SAUCE

1 bacon slice

1 bunch of fresh thyme

Extra-virgin olive oil

½ onion

2 garlic cloves

2 cups ketchup

¼ cup brown sugar

¼ cup molasses

2 tablespoons red or white wine vinegar

1 tablespoon dry mustard

1 teaspoon ground cumin

1 teaspoon smoked paprika

Freshly ground black pepper

Preheat the oven to 250°F. Put the ribs on a baking sheet, stick them in the oven, and let the ribs bake, low and slow, for 1½ hours.

Meanwhile, make the sauce. Wrap the bacon around the thyme bunch and tie with kitchen twine so you have a nice bundle. Heat a 2-count of oil in a large saucepan over medium heat. Add the thyme bundle and cook slowly for 3 to 4 minutes to render the bacon fat and give the sauce a nice smoky taste. Add the onion and garlic and cook slowly without coloring for 5 minutes. Add all of the rest of the sauce ingredients, give the sauce a stir, and turn the heat down to low. Cook slowly for 20 minutes to meld the flavors.

Baste the ribs with the sauce and let them continue cooking, basting twice more, for 30 more minutes. When the ribs are cooked, take them out of the oven. You can let them hang out like this until you're ready to eat.

Preheat an outdoor gas or charcoal grill to medium hot, or preheat a broiler. If you're grilling outside, take a few paper towels and fold them several times to make a thick square. Blot a small amount of oil on the paper towel and carefully and quickly wipe the hot grates of the grill to make a nonstick surface. Throw your ribs on the grill or under the broiler and cook, basting a couple of times with the sauce, until crisp and charred, about 5 minutes on each side. Pick the onion and garlic out of the barbecue sauce and serve with the ribs.

THE ULTIMATE BURGER

FOR BETTER OR FOR WORSE, THE HAMBURGER IS AN ICON OF CLASSIC AMERICAN COOKING. *When it's bad or boring, you shrug it off, but when it's perfect, it's like ending the quest for the holy grail. It's not just a meal, it's an experience.*

I've got a couple of great tips here for perfecting the art of the all-American hamburger. I only use ground brisket, which adds a decent amount of fat and makes the juiciest hamburger I've ever eaten. (Have your friendly butcher do the grinding for you.) But it's not just about the burger—it's also about all the great stuff that goes on top, like crisp pancetta and rosemary, vine-ripened tomatoes marinated with chives and sea salt, juicy sautéed mushrooms, and sweet caramelized onions. Stack it all up together and you elevate the humble burger to a religious experience.

MAKES 8 BURGERS

2 pounds brisket, ground

Kosher salt and freshly ground black pepper

8 thin slices Swiss cheese

8 hamburger buns, split

The Burger Bar fixin's (recipes follow)

Preheat an outdoor gas or charcoal grill to medium hot. Take a few paper towels and fold them several times to make a thick square. Blot a small amount of oil on the paper towel and carefully and quickly wipe the hot grates of the grill to make a nonstick surface.

Season the ground meat in a bowl with salt and pepper. Give it about 3 turns in the bowl with your hands or a big spoon and it's done. Shape into 8 patties. When the grill is hot, put the burgers on the grill and cook for 7 minutes per side for rare or 8 minutes per side for medium, adding the cheese during the final minute or two to melt. Remove the burgers to a plate. Rub the grill with the folded paper towel again to clean it. Then toast the buns cut side down for about 1 minute, just to mark them. Serve the hamburgers in the buns with any of the accompaniments on pages 96–97.

THE BURGER BAR
EVERYTHING YOU NEED TO TOP THE ULTIMATE BURGER

SAUTÉED MUSHROOMS

Sauté 1 pound thickly sliced mushrooms in ¼ cup olive oil with 2 sliced garlic cloves and 1 tablespoon fresh thyme leaves over super-high heat until nicely browned, 8 to 10 minutes. Stir in a couple drops of fresh lemon juice to brighten the flavor.

CARAMELIZED ONIONS

Heat 2 tablespoons unsalted butter with 2 tablespoons olive oil in a large pan over medium heat. Add 2 onions cut into ½-inch-thick slices, sprinkle with salt and pepper, and cook slowly until well caramelized, 15 to 20 minutes.

TOMATOES WITH SEA SALT AND CHIVES

Thickly slice 2 pounds heirloom tomatoes, drizzle with olive oil, and sprinkle with sea salt and ½ bunch of fresh chives, chopped.

PANCETTA CIRCLES WITH ROSEMARY

Lay out ½ pound sliced pancetta on a baking sheet. Strip the leaves from 1 rosemary sprig and throw them on top with lots of cracked black pepper and roast at 400°F until the pancetta is crisp, about 10 minutes.

HERBED HORSERADISH MAYONNAISE

Stir together 1 cup mayonnaise, 1 tablespoon prepared horse-radish, ¼ cup freshly minced herbs such as parsley, basil, or chives, or scallion;, 2 tablespoons of olive oil, a little squeeze of lemon juice, and salt and pepper.

CHILE KETCHUP

Stir enough sambal into ketchup to make it as hot as you like. For starters, try 1 teaspoon sambal to ¼ cup ketchup.

THE ULTIMATE NEW YORK STRIP STEAK WITH BRANDIED MUSHROOMS

NEW YORK STRIP IS MY FAVORITE CUT OF STEAK FOR A COUPLE OF REASONS. *It's an impressive crowd pleaser that really shows your friends you like them a lot; and it takes very little effort to make a New York strip taste delicious.*

If you can find a good meat purveyor who carries dry-aged steaks, it only takes sea salt and freshly ground pepper to really pull out the delicious flavor of the meat. The mushrooms are left whole and sautéed in the residual beef drippings in the bottom of the skillet with lots of fresh thyme and garlic. Finished with brandy and cream, the flavors cook down and meld into a delicious mushroom sauce; poured over the top of the steak, it fits like a well-tailored Armani suit.

SERVES 4

½ cup extra-virgin olive oil

4 boneless New York strip steaks, each about 1½ inches thick

Kosher salt and freshly ground black pepper

2 pounds white mushrooms, caps left whole (don't trim stems!)

Leaves from 2 fresh thyme sprigs

1 tablespoon chopped garlic

¼ cup brandy

½ cup heavy cream

Oven Fries (page 212)

Heat 2 tablespoons of the oil in each of 2 large sauté pans over medium-high heat until smoking. Sprinkle the steaks all over with salt and pepper. Put 2 steaks in each pan and cook, turning to brown all sides completely, until medium-rare, 8 to 10 minutes total. Remove the steaks to a platter with tongs and cover loosely with a tent of aluminum foil to keep the meat warm while you make the sauce.

Put one of the sauté pans back over medium-high heat and add the remaining ¼ cup of olive oil. When the oil is smoking, add the mushrooms and cook, stirring, for about 10 minutes, until golden brown. Then add the thyme and garlic, and season well with salt and pepper. Toss a few more times to cook the garlic, then dump the mushrooms out onto a platter. Take the pan off the heat and add the brandy. Put the pan back on the heat and cook until the brandy is almost evaporated. Add the cream and cook that down for 2 to 3 minutes, until reduced by about half and thickened. Return the mushrooms to the pan with whatever juices have collected on the platter and simmer the whole thing another 2 minutes until thickened again. Season with salt and pepper.

Slice the steaks thin against the grain and serve with the sauce and fries.

GRILLED SKIRT STEAK WITH LENTILS, CILANTRO, AND GREEN GRAPES

LENTILS USUALLY GET CLASSIFIED AS EITHER VEGETARIAN OR . . . VEGETARIAN. *But with chunks of feta cheese, sweet grapes, cilantro, green chile, and lemon, this fresh summer lentil salad has something more going for it. Cool and crisp with the green grapes, and distinctively Latin American in taste, it's a delicious healthy side dish that goes great with grilled skirt steak. I love to use beluga lentils in this recipe. They're available at www.thefoodstores.com or 1-888-EAT-FOOD.*

SERVES 4

1 head of garlic, cut in half through the equator

Kosher salt

Extra-virgin olive oil

3 fresh thyme sprigs

1½ pounds skirt steak

Freshly ground black pepper

LENTIL SALAD

1 cup lentils

1 garlic clove, smashed

1 green chile, finely minced

Grated zest and juice of 1 lemon

Leaves from 1 bunch of fresh cilantro

1 pound green grapes, halved

6 ounces feta cheese, broken into pieces

Cracked black pepper

Preheat the oven to 400°F. Cut a piece of aluminum foil about 12 inches long. Put the halved head of garlic on one half of the foil, sprinkle with salt, drizzle in some olive oil and a couple teaspoons of water, and add 2 of the thyme sprigs. Fold the foil over the garlic to enclose and fold in the ends 2 or 3 times to seal. Put the package in the oven and roast for 30 minutes, or until the garlic is soft.

Preheat an outdoor gas or charcoal grill to medium hot. While the grill heats, take a few paper towels and fold them several times to make a thick square. Blot a small amount of oil on the paper towel and carefully and quickly wipe the hot grates of the grill to make a nonstick surface. Rub the steak all over with olive oil and season generously with salt and ground pepper.

Meanwhile, put the lentils in a saucepan and add cold water to cover by about 2 inches. Add the smashed garlic clove, the remaining thyme sprig, and 1 teaspoon of salt. Bring to a simmer and cook for about 30 minutes, or until the lentils are tender but not mushy. Drain, then discard the garlic and thyme.

When the grill is hot, throw the steak on the grill and cook, turning, until medium-rare, 5 to 7 minutes. Pull the steak off the grill and let rest for 5 minutes.

To serve, dump the lentils into a bowl and add the chile, lemon zest and juice, cilantro, grapes, feta cheese, and ⅓ cup olive oil. Toss and taste for salt. Cut the steak into thin slices. Make a bed of lentils on 4 plates and arrange the steak slices on top. Drizzle the steak slices with olive oil and shower with cracked black pepper. Serve the roasted garlic on the side

THE ULTIMATE SUNDAY DINNER OF MEAT AND POTATOES

I LOVE THE WAY THE DEEP AROMAS OF BRAISED MEAT MAKE THE HOUSE SMELL ON THE WEEKEND. *This recipe is a throwback to my mom's classic pot roast. She would take a top round; put it in her Crock-Pot with onions, a few bay leaves, and lots of black pepper; and let it cook for hours. I've updated her recipe with red wine and lots of fresh thyme and rosemary.*

SERVES 4

Extra-virgin olive oil

3 pounds top round, in one big hunk

Kosher salt and freshly ground black pepper

1 onion, sliced

2 fresh rosemary sprigs

3 fresh thyme sprigs

½ bottle dry red wine that you wouldn't mind drinking

2 cups beef broth

2 bay leaves

Velvet Potato Purée (page 198)

Preheat the oven to 350°F. Heat a 2-count of olive oil in an oven-proof braising pan or Dutch oven over medium-high heat until smoking. Season the meat well with salt and pepper, put it in the pan, and brown for 10 to 12 minutes. Make sure it's really well seared on all sides—this is where the flavor comes from. Take the meat out of the pan and put it on a plate.

Add the onion, rosemary, and thyme to the pan and stir and cook for about 5 minutes to give the onion a good sear. Now add the wine, broth, and bay leaves and bring the whole thing to a simmer. Return the meat to the pan. Cover, put the pan in the oven, and cook until the meat is fork-tender, about 2½ hours.

Remove the meat to a platter. Taste the braising liquid for salt and pepper and discard the bay leaves. Slice the meat and serve in shallow bowls atop a big spoonful of the potato purée. Top with some of the sauce and garnish each bowl with a drizzle of olive oil to finish.

PAN-FRIED LAMB CHOPS WITH HARISSA

MIDDLE EASTERN PREPARATIONS REALLY DO LAMB JUSTICE *because the mellow, gamy taste of the meat stands up to the bright, punchy flavors of that cuisine. One of my favorite condiments is a deep-flavored roasted pepper purée called harissa. It's an interesting sauce made with a bunch of spices that you probably already have in your cupboard: cumin, coriander, and caraway seed.*

SERVES 4

HARISSA

1 teaspoon cumin seeds

1 teaspoon coriander seeds

1 teaspoon caraway seeds

1 small jar roasted red bell peppers, drained

2 garlic cloves

3 small fresh red chiles, chopped

1 teaspoon kosher salt

3 tablespoons extra-virgin olive oil

Juice of 1 lemon

4 tablespoons extra-virgin olive oil

12 fat lamb chops

Kosher salt and freshly ground black pepper

Bulgur Wheat Salad (recipe follows)

First make the harissa: Gather the cumin, coriander, and caraway in a small skillet and toast over low heat until fragrant. Then grind to a powder in a spice mill or a clean coffee grinder. Put the roasted bell peppers into a food processor along with the ground spices, garlic, chiles, salt, olive oil, and lemon juice and pulse to purée.

When you're ready to eat, heat 2 tablespoons olive oil in each of 2 large skillets over medium-high heat. Sprinkle the chops on both sides with salt and pepper. Put the chops in the pans and sear for about 2 minutes on each side to brown. Serve the chops with the harissa and the bulgur salad.

BULGUR WHEAT SALAD (SERVES 4 TO 6)

2½ cups boiling water

1 cup medium-grind bulgur wheat

Kosher salt

Juice of 1 lemon

2 tablespoons extra-virgin olive oil

½ cup smoked or toasted almonds

6 scallions, trimmed and thinly sliced

½ cup chopped fresh flat-leaf parsley

Leaves from 1 bunch of fresh mint

Freshly ground black pepper

8 fresh black Mission figs, cut in half through the stem ends

Pour the boiling water over the bulgur in a heat-proof medium bowl. Stir in ½ teaspoon salt, cover with a piece of plastic wrap, and let stand until the bulgur has absorbed the liquid and is tender, 15 to 20 minutes. If any liquid is left in the bowl, strain the bulgur through a fine sieve. Then stir in the lemon juice and olive oil. Wrap the almonds in a tea towel and crush with a rolling pin or the bottom of a heavy saucepan; stir into the bulgur along with the scallions, parsley, and mint, and season with salt and pepper. Scatter the figs on top.

GRILLED LEG OF LAMB WITH LEMON CHICKPEA PURÉE AND GREENS

A GRILLED LEG OF LAMB SOUNDS INTIMIDATING but it's truly one of the easiest ways to plan dinner for a large group of people. When I buy a leg of lamb, I ask the butcher behind the counter to bone it. Back in my kitchen, I create a classic Greek-style marinade, slather it over the leg of lamb, put it in the fridge, and let it marinate while I heat the grill.

Finishing the leg on the grill takes two hands and two tongs, but it's just as easy as grilling a big steak. I think lamb is best cooked a little beyond rare; at medium or even medium-rare, the fat gets a chance to melt into the succulent meat. Stick an instant-read thermometer into the thickest part of the leg; when it registers 130°F, the meat will be nice and juicy. Make sure to let it rest after you cook it; and slice it thin, against the grain.

The Lemon Chickpea Purée is fairly simply made by doctoring canned chickpeas with lemon juice, lemon zest, and lots of extra-virgin olive oil.

SERVES 6 TO 8

½ cup extra-virgin olive oil

¼ cup red wine vinegar

4 garlic cloves, chopped

2 tablespoons fresh oregano, chopped

1 tablespoon fresh thyme leaves

Juice of 1 lemon

Kosher salt and freshly ground black pepper

1 (3½-pound) boneless leg of lamb, butterflied but not tied

1 bunch of mâche or baby greens

Leaves from 1 bunch of fresh mint

2 scallions, sliced thin

Lemon Chickpea Purée (recipe follows)

To make the vinaigrette, whisk together the oil, vinegar, garlic, oregano, thyme, and lemon juice in a bowl; season with salt and pepper. Pat the lamb dry and put it on a shallow platter. Season all over with salt and pepper. Pour half of the vinaigrette over the lamb and turn the meat to get it well coated. Let it marinate while you heat the grill, or refrigerate for up to 2 hours.

Preheat an outdoor gas or charcoal grill to medium hot. Take a few paper towels and fold them several times to make a thick square. Blot a small amount of oil on the paper towel and carefully and quickly wipe the hot grates of the grill to make a nonstick surface.

Put the lamb on the grill and cook for 15 to 20 minutes on each side for medium-rare. Transfer to a cutting board, cover with foil, and let rest for 10 minutes.

To serve, toss the mâche, mint leaves, and scallions in a bowl. Dress with about 3 tablespoons of the remaining vinaigrette and season with salt and pepper. Slice the lamb and serve with the greens and the chickpea purée; drizzle with the rest of the vinaigrette.

LEMON CHICKPEA PURÉE (SERVES 6 TO 8)

1 large can (28 ounces) chickpeas, drained

Extra-virgin olive oil

Zest and juice of 3 lemons

2 garlic cloves, finely minced

Kosher salt and freshly ground black pepper

1 tablespoon chopped fresh flat-leaf parsley

Put the chickpeas into a food processor or blender with ½ cup olive oil, the lemon zest and juice, garlic, and salt and pepper to taste. Process until smooth, thinning with a little water if the mixture is too stiff to purée. Scrape out into a bowl, drizzle with a little more olive oil, and sprinkle with parsley.

JUICY GRILLED PORK CHOPS WITH BLACK OLIVE TAPENADE AND ROASTED VINE TOMATOES

THIS IS FARMSTAND COOKING AT ITS FINEST: *The roasted squash and tomatoes taste like vacation. The vegetables get tossed with parsley, lots of extra-virgin olive oil, salt, and pepper, then are roasted in the oven until the tomatoes burst, creating a juicy side dish that's full of flavor and super healthy.*

Brining pork chops is an old restaurant trick that I use to ensure that everybody gets a juicy chop, and my method only takes about a half hour. The salty black olive tapenade ties the pork and vegetables together and any leftover tapenade is great for antipasto, smeared on a toasted crostini.

SERVES 4

PORK CHOPS

2 quarts water

¼ cup sugar

¼ cup kosher salt

4 fresh thyme sprigs

4 bone-in pork chops, about 1½ inches thick

BLACK OLIVE TAPENADE

1 cup pitted kalamata olives

2 anchovy fillets

1 small garlic clove

Pinch of crushed red pepper flakes

Small handful of fresh flat-leaf parsley

1 tablespoon red or white wine vinegar

3 tablespoons extra-virgin olive oil

Kosher salt and freshly ground black pepper

Extra-virgin olive oil

Kosher salt and freshly ground black pepper

Roasted Summer Squash (recipe follows)

Basil leaves or watercress sprigs, for garnish

For the pork, combine the water, sugar, salt, and thyme sprigs in a gallon-size resealable bag. Add the pork chops, seal up the bag, and put it in the refrigerator for about 30 minutes while you make the tapenade.

Put the olives, anchovies, garlic, red pepper flakes, parsley, vinegar, and olive oil in a food processor or blender and process to a coarse purée. Season with salt, if needed, and black pepper and set aside.

Now preheat an outdoor gas or charcoal grill to a medium-high heat. While the grill heats, take a few paper towels and fold them several times to make a thick square. Blot a small amount of oil on the paper towel and carefully and quickly wipe the hot grates of the grill to make a nonstick surface.

Take the pork out of the brine and pat it dry. Rub the pork all over with olive oil and sprinkle with salt and pepper. Grill over medium-high heat for 5 to 7 minutes on each side, until the chops are well browned and still rosy in the center and register 140°F when tested with an instant-read thermometer. To serve, spoon some squash onto the plates and put the pork chops on top. Drizzle with the tapenade and garnish with basil or watercress.

ROASTED SUMMER VEGETABLES (SERVES 4)

¾ pound zucchini, sliced ½ inch thick

¾ pound summer squash, sliced ½ inch thick

1 cup cherry tomatoes

¼ cup chopped fresh flat-leaf parsley

Kosher salt and freshly ground black pepper

¼ cup extra-virgin olive oil

Preheat the oven to 425°F. Throw the zucchini, summer squash, tomatoes, and parsley into a medium roasting pan. Sprinkle with salt and pepper. Add the olive oil and toss to coat the vegetables. Stick that in the oven and roast for 20 to 25 minutes, until the vegetables are soft—Grandma-style—and beginning to brown.

GRILLED PORK TENDERLOIN WITH CHILE-COCONUT SAUCE

I REALLY LOVE THIS DISH. *It's a fresh summer salad using pork tenderloin, a cut that everyone's cooking these days. The coconut dressing on the tomato salad has a deep, explosive flavor borrowed from Thailand and the ingredients are easy to find at your local grocery.*

If you're a big fan of Asian cooking like I am, you'll do yourself a favor by having some Asian ingredients on hand: Fresh ginger and chiles, coconut milk, lemongrass, and fish sauce are the base for lots of other Thai dishes. And once you taste this simple salad, you'll think about it every time you see a basket of lemongrass at the produce counter of your grocery store.

SERVES 4

PORK TENDERLOIN

2 pork tenderloins, 1½ to 2 pounds total

Kosher salt and freshly ground black pepper

¼ cup extra-virgin olive oil

Juice of ½ lime

CHILE–COCONUT SAUCE

2 tablespoons extra-virgin olive oil

1-inch piece of fresh ginger, peeled and chopped

2 garlic cloves, chopped

1 lemongrass stalk, white part only, chopped into small pieces

1 fresh Thai bird chile, cut into rounds

Stems from ¼ bunch of fresh cilantro

1 can (14 ounces) unsweetened coconut milk

1 teaspoon sugar

Juice of 1 lime

1 tablespoon fish sauce (nam pla)

Kosher salt and freshly ground black pepper

Coconut-Tomato Salad (recipe follows)

Put the pork on a platter and sprinkle all over with salt and pepper. Add the olive oil and lime juice and turn to coat the pork with the marinade. Cover with plastic wrap and set aside in the refrigerator.

For the chile–coconut sauce, heat the olive oil in a saucepan over medium heat. Add the ginger, garlic, lemongrass, chile, and cilantro stems and cook to soften, about 3 minutes. Add the coconut milk and sugar and simmer until thickened, about 5 minutes. Squeeze in the lime juice and season with the fish sauce, salt, and pepper. Cool to room temperature.

Preheat an outdoor gas or charcoal grill. Blot some oil onto a thick square of paper towel and then carefully and quickly wipe the hot grates of the grill to make a nonstick surface. Put the pork on the grill and cook, turning to brown all sides, until crusty on the outside and almost cooked through but still slightly pink in the center, 10 to 15 minutes. Remove from the grill and let rest for a few minutes.

To serve, slice the pork and add it to the bowl with the tomato salad. Pour over the chile–coconut sauce and toss it all together.

COCONUT–TOMATO SALAD (SERVES 4)

1½ cups shredded, unsweetened coconut

2 pounds fresh heirloom tomatoes, cut into big chunks (use a variety of colors—purple, yellow, bright red)

½ small red onion, slivered

1 fresh Thai bird chile, thinly sliced

Leaves from ¼ bunch of fresh cilantro

Handful of fresh mint leaves

Kosher salt and freshly ground black pepper

Extra-virgin olive oil

2 scallions, trimmed and chopped

Preheat the oven to 375°F. Spread the coconut out in a thin layer on a baking sheet and bake, shaking every now and then for even cooking, until lightly browned, about 10 minutes.

In a big bowl, toss together the tomatoes, red onion, chile, cilantro, mint, and salt and pepper. Drizzle with olive oil and fold in the toasty coconut and scallions.

PAN-FRIED SAUSAGE WITH APPLES, POTATOES, AND CABBAGE

THIS IS A CLASSIC FRENCH BISTRO DISH THAT I'VE EATEN A COUPLE OF TIMES *on my travels in Europe, and I love to make it at home. You can use any style sausage you like, from classic* boudin blanc *to* kielbasa—*it all works. The caramelized apples and cabbage are a perfect bittersweet yin and yang. It's a fantastic dish to pair with a great glass of wine on a chilly day.*

SERVES 4

Kosher salt

Extra-virgin olive oil

1½ pounds fat pork sausages

2 Golden Delicious apples, peeled, halved, cored, and cut into wedges

2 teaspoons brown sugar

1 teaspoon fresh thyme leaves

7 tablespoons unsalted butter

1 tablespoon vinegar (any kind will do)

1 large head Savoy cabbage, quartered, cored, leaves separated and torn into large pieces

2 tablespoons chopped fresh flat-leaf parsley

½ bunch of fresh chives, chopped

Freshly ground black pepper

Velvet Potato Purée (page 198)

Bring a big pot of salted water to a boil over high heat for the cabbage.

Heat a 2-count of oil in a large skillet over medium heat. Add the sausages and cook until nicely browned on the outside and cooked through, about 15 minutes. Transfer the sausages to a platter. Add the apples to the pan and sprinkle with the brown sugar and the thyme. Add 3 tablespoons of the butter, raise the heat to medium-high, and cook until the apples are wilted and caramelized, 4 to 5 minutes. Dump the apples out onto the platter with the sausages.

By now your water should be boiling. Add the vinegar and then the cabbage and boil over high heat until the cabbage is wilted (don't overcook it—it should still have tooth), 2 to 3 minutes. Drain, then toss in a bowl with the remaining 4 tablespoons butter, the parsley, chives, and salt and pepper. Serve the sausages and apples with the cabbage and potato purée.

rds

When it comes to cooking dinner for your family, let's face it: Chicken makes the world go 'round. It's easy to get your hands on, it's inexpensive, and everybody loves it. You may have noticed, though, that the poultry section of the market has been growing with organic turkey, duck, and Cornish hens: There's a lot more to choose from these days. This chapter will help you navigate it all, from a classic roasted chicken with a Provençal twist to a simple, Asian-inspired duck dish and the only barbecued chicken recipe you'll ever need. Here's a collection of recipes that will give you a fresh perspective at the poultry counter and put a smile on your face when your house smells great.

GRILLED CHICKEN WITH GARLIC-HERB DRESSING AND GRILLED LEMON

THIS IS THE PERFECT GRILLED CHICKEN RECIPE; YOU SHOULD TRY IT FOR THE DRESSING ALONE. *It's a thick purée of sweet roasted garlic, lemon, olive oil, and fresh herbs and it's bright green, like a pesto. You grill the chicken until the skin is crisp and then right at the end, finish it off with the fresh flavors of the dressing. Backed up by some of the picnic side dishes in the Garden chapter (see page 178), it tastes like the ultimate summertime party.*

SERVES 4

1 head of garlic, cut in half at the equator

Kosher salt

Extra-virgin olive oil

2 whole fresh thyme sprigs, plus leaves from 6 sprigs

Juice of 2 lemons, plus 2 lemons, halved

½ cup chopped fresh flat-leaf parsley

1 (4- to 4½-pound) chicken, cut into 10 pieces

Freshly ground black pepper

1 medium head of radicchio, preferably Treviso, cut into quarters

Preheat the oven to 400°F. Cut a piece of aluminum foil about 12 inches long. Put the garlic on one half of the foil, sprinkle with salt, drizzle in some olive oil and a couple of teaspoons of water, and add the 2 sprigs of thyme. Fold the foil over the garlic to enclose and fold in the edges 2 or 3 times to seal. Put the package in the oven and roast for 30 minutes, or until the garlic is soft. Open the package and let the garlic cool a bit, then squeeze out the cloves into a food processor or blender. Add ½ cup olive oil, the lemon juice, parsley, and thyme leaves and purée to make a thick vinaigrette.

Preheat an outdoor gas or charcoal grill to medium hot.

Rinse the chicken and pat dry with paper towels. Put the pieces in a bowl, sprinkle with salt and pepper, and drizzle with olive oil; toss to coat with the seasonings and then refrigerate while you get everything else together. Put the radicchio in another bowl, drizzle with olive oil, sprinkle with salt and pepper, and toss; set that aside.

When you're ready to cook, take a few paper towels and fold them several times to make a thick square. Blot a small amount of oil on the paper towel and carefully and quickly wipe the hot grates of the grill to make a nonstick surface. Put the chicken on the grill, skin side down, along with the radicchio quarters and grill them together. Cook the radicchio for about 2 minutes per side until it has a nice char; pull it off the grill and set aside to cool. Grill the chicken for 20 minutes, turning once, then baste with about half of the vinaigrette and keep cooking until an instant-read thermometer stuck into the thickest part of the thigh reads 160°F and the chicken is nice and caramelized all over, 15 to 20 more minutes. During the last few minutes, throw the lemon halves on the grill, cut sides down, and cook until just marked and smoky.

To serve, separate the radicchio into individual leaves in a big bowl. Add the chicken and the rest of the dressing and toss well. Serve with grilled lemon halves and squeeze the lemon all over the chicken.

GRILLED CHICKEN WITH PEACH BARBECUE SAUCE

THE SIMPLE PROCESS OF BRINING TAKES BARBECUED CHICKEN FROM PEDESTRIAN TO MOUTHWATERING *in as little as fifteen minutes. And the sauce . . . bring an extra stack of napkins because you're going to be licking it off your elbows! It's a peach-flavored twist on the original and it's amazing.*

SERVES 4 TO 6

BRINE

2 quarts water

2 tablespoons kosher salt

¼ cup brown sugar

2 garlic cloves, smashed with the side of a large knife

4 fresh thyme sprigs

2 (3½- to 4-pound) chickens, quartered

PEACH BARBECUE SAUCE

1 bacon slice

1 bunch of fresh thyme

Extra-virgin olive oil

½ onion

2 garlic cloves

2 cups ketchup

1 cup peach preserves

¼ cup brown sugar

¼ cup molasses

2 tablespoons red or white wine vinegar

1 tablespoon dry mustard

1 teaspoon ground cumin

1 teaspoon smoked paprika

Freshly ground black pepper

For the brine, combine the water, salt, sugar, garlic, and thyme in a 2-gallon resealable plastic bag. Add the chicken, close the bag, and refrigerate for up to 2 hours (if you've only got 15 minutes, that's fine) to allow the salt and seasonings to penetrate the chicken.

Meanwhile, make the sauce. Wrap the bacon around the thyme bunch and tie with kitchen twine so you have a nice bundle. Heat a 2-count of oil in a large saucepan over medium heat. Add the thyme bundle and cook slowly for 3 to 4 minutes to render the bacon fat and give the sauce a nice smoky taste. Add the onion and garlic and cook slowly without coloring for 5 minutes. Add all of the rest of the sauce ingredients, give the sauce a stir, and turn the heat down to low. Cook slowly for 20 minutes to meld the flavors.

Preheat an outdoor gas or charcoal grill to medium hot. Take a few paper towels and fold them several times to make a thick square. Blot a small amount of oil on the paper towel and carefully and quickly wipe the hot grates of the grill to make a nonstick surface. Take the chicken out of the brine, pat it dry with paper towels, and cook, turning once, for 15 minutes. Brush the chicken with the sauce and continue cooking until the chicken is cooked through, 5 to 10 more minutes. Serve with extra sauce.

LEMON CURRY CHICKEN

HERE'S BRILLIANT, SIMPLE COOKING WITH AN INDIAN TWIST. *The flavors of yogurt, curry powder, and sesame oil make a delicious marinade that tenderizes the chicken and keeps it juicy; roasting on a sheet pan couldn't be easier. Sweet mango, crunchy cashews, and fresh mint folded into fragrant basmati rice makes a fresh, healthy rice salad full of bright flavors and you can get dinner on the table in under an hour.*

SERVES 4

1 (3½- to 4-pound) chicken, cut into 10 pieces

2 cups plain yogurt
2 tablespoons curry powder
Grated zest and juice of 1 lemon
1 tablespoon toasted sesame oil
Kosher salt and freshly ground black pepper

Mango–Basmati Rice Salad (recipe follows)

Preheat the oven to 400°F. Rinse the chicken and pat it dry with paper towels. Stir together the yogurt, curry powder, lemon zest and juice, sesame oil, and salt and pepper in a big bowl. Add the chicken and toss gently to coat with the yogurt marinade. Put the chicken on a baking sheet and roast, using the remaining marinade to baste twice as it cooks, until the chicken is tender and cooked through, about 45 minutes total.

Mound the rice salad on a platter. Arrange the chicken on top.

MANGO–BASMATI RICE SALAD (SERVES 4)

1 cup basmati rice
1-inch piece of fresh ginger, peeled and smashed with the flat side of a large knife
Kosher salt
½ pound tender green beans, trimmed
½ small red onion
¼ cup cashews
¼ cup fresh mint leaves
1 fresh mango, peeled, pitted, and chopped
2 tablespoons extra-virgin olive oil
Juice of ½ lemon
Freshly ground black pepper

Put the rice into a saucepan with the ginger, 2 cups of water, and 1½ teaspoons salt and bring to a simmer over medium heat. Give the rice a stir, turn the heat down to low, cover, and cook for 12 minutes without lifting the lid. Spread the cooked rice out on a baking sheet and let it cool to room temperature. Discard the ginger.

Bring a large pot of salted water to a boil for the beans. Fill a large bowl with ice water and add enough salt to make it taste lightly salted. Add the beans to the boiling water and cook until just tender, about 3 minutes. Drain, then refresh in the ice-water bath to keep the bright green color, and drain well again. Cut the beans in half crosswise on the diagonal.

Put the onion half, the cashews, and mint on a cutting board and coarsely chop them all up. Combine the rice and green beans in a big bowl and add the chopped onion mixture. Add the chopped mango, olive oil, and lemon juice and toss gently. Taste for seasoning.

SESAME CHICKEN SALAD WITH SPINACH, CUCUMBER, AND CILANTRO

THE ASIAN-INSPIRED DRESSING ON THIS SUBSTANTIAL SALAD HITS YOUR TONGUE IN SEVERAL DIFFERENT PLACES—*spicy, sour, salty, and sweet notes. It makes a great lunch or light dinner.*

SERVES 4

VINAIGRETTE

¼ cup soy sauce

Juice of ½ lemon

1 tablespoon rice wine vinegar

⅓ cup extra-virgin olive oil

1-inch piece of fresh ginger, peeled and chopped

1 teaspoon sugar

1 teaspoon crushed red pepper flakes

¼ cup plus 2 tablespoons sesame seeds

4 boneless, skinless chicken breasts (about 1½ pounds)

1½ cups panko (Japanese bread crumbs)

Kosher salt and freshly ground black pepper

⅓ cup extra-virgin olive oil

A couple good handfuls of stemmed spinach leaves (about 4 cups)

1 cucumber, unpeeled, cut crosswise into thin slices

Handful of fresh cilantro leaves

1 scallion, white and green part, sliced

Cracked black pepper

In a bowl, whisk together the soy sauce, lemon juice, vinegar, olive oil, ginger, sugar, and red pepper flakes for the vinaigrette.

Toast 2 tablespoons of the sesame seeds in a small dry skillet until fragrant, a minute or two, then set aside.

Rinse the chicken and pat dry with paper towels. Put a chicken breast on the cutting board and, holding a large knife parallel to the board, cut through the breast horizontally so that you get 2 thin fillets. Repeat with the 3 remaining breasts. Put the chicken on a platter, drizzle with 2 tablespoons of the vinaigrette, and toss to coat. Set the rest of the vinaigrette aside. Let the chicken marinate for about 10 minutes.

Combine the panko and the remaining ¼ cup sesame seeds in a shallow bowl and season with a little salt and pepper. Mix with your fingers so that the seasoning is incorporated and then taste it; the panko should be well seasoned. Dredge the chicken in the seasoned crumbs, patting the crumbs gently so that they adhere.

Heat the olive oil in a large skillet over medium-high heat. Line a platter with paper towels and set that to the side of the stove. Add about half of the chicken to the pan and cook about 2 minutes on each side, until golden brown and crispy. Remove the chicken to the towel-lined platter to drain while you cook the rest of the chicken.

Put the spinach in a bowl with the cucumber, cilantro, scallion, and a tablespoon of the toasted sesame seeds, and give it a good toss. To serve, arrange a mound of greens on a plate, set a piece of chicken on top, stack a few more greens on top, and finish with another piece of chicken. Drizzle with vinaigrette. Make 3 more plates this way and shower with the remaining tablespoon of toasted sesame seeds and cracked black pepper.

CHICKEN AND COCONUT "PAELLA"

THIS IS ONE OF THOSE DELICIOUS HODGEPODGE DISHES
THAT DEFIES DESCRIPTION: *Despite the ingredients, it's not
really Spanish though it is reminiscent of a paella, nor is it
Asian, and it's definitely not Italian. Chicken thighs,
lightly crusted with crushed coriander seeds, develop a deep,
lemony aroma when sautéed. The thighs get tucked into
basmati rice that has been simmered in sweet coconut milk
and ginger. The dish is finished in the oven and then goes
straight out to the table and served family style.*

SERVES 4 TO 6

1/4 cup coriander seeds

8 chicken thighs

Kosher salt and freshly ground black pepper

Extra-virgin olive oil

1 onion, finely minced

1-inch piece of fresh ginger, peeled and chopped

1 bay leaf

2 cups basmati rice

Grated zest of 1 lemon

1 1/2 cups chicken broth

1 1/2 cups coconut milk

PEA SALAD

1 cup frozen green peas, thawed in a colander under cool water

Small handful of fresh mint leaves

1 bunch of watercress

Juice of 1/2 lemon

3 tablespoons extra-virgin olive oil

Kosher salt and freshly ground black pepper

Mint leaves, for garnish

Lemon wedges, for garnish

Preheat the oven to 400°F. Coarsely crack the coriander in one of three ways: pulse in a spice grinder; wrap the seeds in a tea towel and crush with a rolling pin or the bottom of a heavy pan; or grind in a pepper grinder on the coarse setting. Season the thighs well with salt and pepper and sprinkle all over with the cracked coriander. Heat a 3-count of olive oil in a large, deep, ovenproof skillet over medium-high heat. Lay the chicken thighs in the pan, skin side down, and give them a good sear for 3 to 4 minutes to develop a nice crust. Turn and cook for 3 to 4 minutes on the other side to brown the meat. Take the chicken out of the pan.

Hit the pan with another tablespoon of olive oil and turn the heat down to medium. Add the onion, ginger, and bay leaf and cook, stirring, for 3 to 4 minutes, until the onion is soft but not colored. Now you've got all this great flavor going on in the bottom of the pan—chicken drippings, ginger, onion, and bay. Add the rice and season with salt and pepper. Stir for a minute or two until the grains are well coated with the oil. Stir in the lemon zest. Now add the broth and coconut milk and bring that to a simmer. Tuck in the chicken thighs, put the whole thing in the oven, and bake, uncovered, until the rice is tender and bound by a creamy sauce and the chicken is entirely cooked through, about 30 minutes. Discard the bay leaf.

When the chicken is done, put the peas, mint, and watercress into a bowl. Add the lemon juice, olive oil, and salt and pepper and give it a good toss. Taste for seasoning. To serve, take a big spoon and scoop out some rice and chicken onto each of 4 plates. Garnish each plate with the pea salad.

THE ULTIMATE ROAST CHICKEN PROVENÇAL

THIS IS, WITHOUT QUESTION, THE BEST ROASTED CHICKEN RECIPE I'VE EVER TASTED, WITH PROVENÇAL FLAVORS INSIDE AND OUT. *The genius of Provençal cooking is that ingredients and cooking methods are simple but when the flavors of the tomatoes, lemons, zucchini, and herbs all melt together, they create a taste that is truly mind-blowing and quintessentially French.*

SERVES 4

HERB PASTE

Leaves from 1 bunch of fresh flat-leaf parsley

Leaves from ¼ bunch of fresh thyme

Leaves from 1 bunch of fresh tarragon

4 garlic cloves

¼ cup extra-virgin olive oil

Kosher salt and freshly ground black pepper

1 whole (3½-pound) chicken

Kosher salt and freshly ground black pepper

1 lemon, cut in half, plus ½ lemon sliced paper-thin

3 big tomatoes, cut into wedges

4 small zucchini, cut into ½-inch-thick rounds

1 red onion, thinly sliced

Leaves from 4 fresh thyme sprigs

Extra-virgin olive oil

Preheat the oven to 400°F.

Throw the parsley, thyme, tarragon, garlic, and olive oil in a blender, season well with salt and pepper, and purée to a green paste.

Rinse the chicken with cool water inside and out and pat dry with paper towels. Set the chicken on a cutting board, and season the cavity generously with salt and pepper. Stuff the lemon halves into the cavity. Fold the wing tips under the bird and tie the legs together with kitchen string to give it a nice shape while it cooks. Rub the chicken all over with the herb paste so it's well coated.

Put the chicken in a large roasting pan fitted with a rack and scatter the tomatoes, zucchini, onion, lemon slices, and thyme around. Give the vegetables a big, healthy dose of olive oil—¼ cup should do it—and sprinkle with salt and pepper. Put the chicken into the oven and roast for 1 hour, then check on it with an instant-read thermometer by popping it into the thickest part of the thigh. When it reads 160°F, the bird is cooked.

Take the pan out of the oven and let the chicken rest for about 10 minutes before carving so the juices have a chance to settle back into the meat. Serve with the roasted vegetables.

OVEN-ROASTED TURKEY BREAST WITH LEEKS AND DRIED FRUIT

I DON'T UNDERSTAND WHY PEOPLE AREN'T COOKING TURKEY MORE OFTEN. *It's lean, it's healthy, and it's really easy to cook. With a sharp knife, I slice into the turkey breast, open it like a book, and stuff it with sautéed leeks and dried fruit, then roll it up again. It cooks in about twenty minutes and it's like having Thanksgiving on an everyday basis. Serve with Velvet Potato Purée on page 198.*

In this recipe I use just one half of a whole breast, saving the other half for another meal or to freeze. If you aren't comfortable boning out the breasts yourself, ask your butcher to do it for you.

SERVES 6 TO 8

4 whole leeks, roots trimmed

2 tablespoons unsalted butter

2 tablespoons extra-virgin olive oil

Leaves from 2 fresh thyme sprigs

Kosher salt and freshly ground black pepper

1 whole (5- to 6-pound) turkey breast on the bone

¼ cup raisins

¼ cup golden raisins

½ cup dried apricots, halved

Trim off most of the dark green part of the leeks, leaving the white and just an inch or two of the light green part. Cut the leeks almost in half lengthwise, leaving the halves attached at the root end. Rinse under cool running water, separating the leaves gently to rinse out the sand that hides in there. Pat the leeks dry. Heat 1 tablespoon each of butter and olive oil in a roasting pan over medium heat. Add the leeks, sprinkle with the thyme, salt, and pepper, and cook for about 10 minutes, turning every now and then, until the leeks are softened but not colored. Pull the leeks out of the pan and let them cool.

Meanwhile, use a sharp, thin knife to cut down the length of the turkey breastbone. Then, holding the knife as flat as possible against the bone, follow the shape of the carcass to cut one breast off the bone. Do the same for the second breast. Wrap 1 breast in plastic and refrigerate or freeze for another use. Butterfly the remaining breast: Put it on a cutting board so that it lies vertically, skin side down. Get yourself a large knife. Cutting parallel to the cutting board, cut the breast almost in half, just stopping short of the outside edge. Open out the 2 halves as if you were opening a book. Now you've got a large piece of meat that will cook evenly and is thin enough to roll.

Preheat the oven to 400°F.

Sprinkle the cut surface of the turkey with salt and pepper and lay the leeks vertically, side by side, on the left side. Scatter the dried fruit over the leeks. Now, starting with the left side, roll the turkey over the filling and into a cylinder. Tie in 4 places with kitchen twine. Season with salt and pepper. (See pages 136–137 for step-by-step photographs of this process.)

Heat the remaining tablespoon of butter and olive oil in the same roasting pan over medium-high heat. Put the turkey in the roasting pan and sear all over. Transfer the pan to the oven and roast for about 20 minutes, until an instant-read thermometer stuck into the meat registers 160°F. Take the turkey out of the oven, let it rest for 5 to 10 minutes, then cut crosswise into slices.

2

3

1. Arrange the filling ingredients vertically across the center of the butterflied breast.

2. Pull one side of the breast up and over the filling, tucking the end tightly into the center.

3. Continue rolling the stuffed breast, making certain that the filling is completely enclosed. Place the roll seam side down on the work surface.

4. Cut 4 lengths of kitchen string and slip them underneath the rolled breast. Tie at 4 even intervals to create a uniform, neat roll.

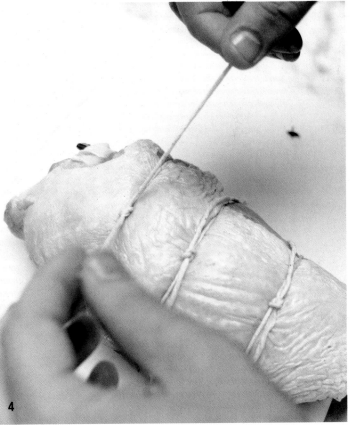

4

CHICKEN PAILLARD WITH FRESH FIG SALAD AND BLUE CHEESE

POUNDING CHICKEN BREASTS INTO PAILLARDS, WHICH MEANS THIN SLICES, IS A GREAT WAY TO USE CHICKEN BREASTS IN THE SUMMERTIME FOR SALAD. *It cooks fast and evenly so the meat stays nice and moist. The salty-sweet combination of figs, pancetta, and blue cheese is dynamite. If you can't get your hands on fresh figs, peaches work just as well.*

SERVES 4

VINAIGRETTE

3 tablespoons honey

¼ cup extra-virgin olive oil

1 shallot, chopped

1 tablespoon sherry vinegar

Juice of ½ lemon

1 teaspoon chopped fresh tarragon

Kosher salt and freshly ground black pepper

4 boneless, skinless chicken breasts (about 1½ pounds)

Kosher salt and freshly ground black pepper

½ pound pancetta

Extra-virgin olive oil

¼ pound blue cheese, broken into hunks

1 bunch of arugula, trimmed

1 small basket seasonal figs, halved

Tarragon leaves, for garnish

First whisk together all of the ingredients for the vinaigrette in a small bowl and set it aside.

Sandwich the chicken breasts between 2 layers of plastic wrap and pound them very thin with the side of a meat cleaver or a rolling pin. Remove the chicken breasts from the plastic and season well on both sides with salt and pepper.

Heat a large sauté pan over medium heat. Unroll the pancetta so it looks like big strips of bacon. Add it to the pan and fry it like a tangle of bacon until the fat is rendered, 3 to 4 minutes. Drain on paper towels.

Drizzle a 2-count of olive oil into the pan with the pancetta drippings. Add the chicken and pan-fry for 3 to 4 minutes on each side to brown the breasts and cook them through. Use a spatula to remove the chicken to the paper towels with the pancetta. Add the vinaigrette to the sauté pan and heat for a few minutes, stirring, to deglaze the bits of pancetta and chicken from the bottom of the pan; take the pan off the heat.

To serve, arrange the chicken on a platter. Scatter the blue cheese, arugula, figs, and pancetta over. Drizzle the dressing over everything and garnish with the tarragon leaves.

THE ULTIMATE FRIED CHICKEN

ONE OF THE BEST CHEFS IN NEW YORK—AND A MAD TUSCAN, TOO—IS A GOOD FRIEND OF MINE NAMED CESARE CASELLA. *Halfway through dinner at his restaurant Beppe one night he sent fried chicken to the table, and I thought for a second he was taking a playful jab at me because of my southern roots. But then he came out and told me a story about how Tuscans had actually invented fried chicken. And having tasted it, I have to say he might be right. This recipe with herbs and garlic kicks the pants off of any fried chicken I've ever tasted.*

SERVES 4

1 (3½-pound) chicken, cut into 10 pieces
Juice of 2 lemons

1 gallon peanut oil, for deep-frying
¼ bunch of fresh thyme
3 big fresh rosemary sprigs
¼ bunch of fresh sage
2 fresh bay leaves
½ head of garlic, smashed, husk still attached

2 cups all-purpose flour
Sea salt and cracked black pepper
4 large eggs
Extra-virgin olive oil
Lemon wedges, for serving

Rinse the chicken pieces and pat dry. Put them in a large bowl and squeeze the lemon juice over them, turning the chicken so that the lemon gets all through it. Let it marinate while you heat the oil.

Pour the peanut oil into a large pasta pot. Add the herbs and garlic and heat over medium-high heat until the oil registers 350°F on one of those clip-on deep-fry thermometers. The herbs and garlic will perfume the oil with their flavor as the oil comes up to temperature.

Meanwhile, put the flour in a large, shallow platter and hit it with a generous seasoning of salt and pepper. Use your fingers to mix the flour with the salt and pepper and then taste it; you should be able to taste the salt and pepper. Crack the eggs into a large, shallow bowl; add a drizzle of olive oil and a couple of tablespoons of water and whisk it all together with a fork.

When the oil reaches 350°F, skim off the herbs and garlic with a slotted spoon; reserve. Roll the chicken pieces around in the seasoned flour until well coated. Shake off the excess, then dunk them into the egg wash. Carefully drop the chicken into the hot oil (you can cook it all at the same time) and cook for about 20 minutes, turning it with tongs every now and then to keep the color even. The chicken is done when the skin is crisp and golden brown and the chicken floats at the surface of the oil. Keep an eye on the temperature and adjust the heat to keep the temperature as even as possible.

When the chicken is done, take a big skimmer and remove all of it from the pot, shaking off as much oil as you can, and lay it on a tea towel or brown paper bag to soak up the oil. Sprinkle all over with more salt and a dusting of cracked black pepper. Scatter the reserved herbs and garlic over the top. Serve hot, with big lemon wedges.

CHICKEN THIGHS WITH WIDE BUTTERED NOODLES, FENNEL, AND GRAPES

THIS IS BASICALLY A VERY SIMPLE BUTTERED NOODLE DISH *with a great chicken component. Chicken thighs, which I think are the best-tasting part of the bird, are seasoned with peppercorns and fennel seeds and roasted with fresh fennel. Those two flavors alone—fennel and chicken—make a delicious dish but I take it one step further by adding crunchy fresh red grapes. The sweet fruit balances out the spicy peppercorns and fennel seed and you've got a really easy noodle dish that's always impressive.*

SERVES 4

Kosher salt

1 tablespoon peppercorns

1 tablespoon fennel seeds

8 chicken thighs

3 tablespoons extra-virgin olive oil

4 small fennel bulbs, trimmed, and split in half through the root ends

1 pound wide egg noodles

4 tablespoons (½ stick) unsalted butter

1 cup halved red grapes

Handful of whole fresh flat-leaf parsley leaves

Preheat the oven to 375°F. Bring a big pot of salted water to a boil for the noodles.

Put the peppercorns and fennel seeds into a spice grinder or a clean coffee grinder and grind to a powder. Sprinkle the chicken thighs all over with the mixture, then sprinkle with salt.

Put an ovenproof skillet large enough to hold the chicken and fennel in a single layer over medium heat. Add the olive oil and heat until almost smoking. Put the chicken in the pan, skin side down, then add the fennel, cut side down. Cook for about 5 minutes, until the skin of the chicken crisps and the fennel turns golden brown. Then turn and cook until both are well browned on the other side, another 5 to 7 minutes. Now turn the chicken and fennel again, throw the pan in the oven, and bake for 30 minutes. Test the chicken by sticking a paring knife into the flesh near the bone: The juices should run clear. If they're pink, put the pan back in the oven for another 5 minutes.

Meanwhile, your pasta water will have come to a boil. Add the noodles, give them a stir to keep them from sticking together, and cook for 8 to 9 minutes, until al dente. Ladle out about 1 cup of the starchy pasta cooking water and reserve, then drain the pasta.

When the chicken comes out of the oven, put it and the fennel on a serving plate, leaving the juices in the pan. Now add the reserved pasta water to the pan and boil over medium-high heat, scraping the bottom of the pan with a wooden spoon to deglaze the caramelized juices. Add the butter and reduce by about half so that you have a nice thick sauce. Add the cooked noodles, the grapes, and the parsley to the skillet and toss that all around to coat the noodles with the sauce. Taste for salt and serve with the chicken.

DUCK STEAKS WITH ROASTED PEACHES AND COLD SESAME NOODLES

THE BEST WAY TO COOK A DUCK BREAST IS TO SCORE THE SKIN WITH A SHARP KNIFE *into a thousand tiny x's and then cook the breast in a dry pan over low heat, skin side down, to render the fat just like you're cooking bacon. This way, the skin gets very crisp and most of the fat will render out by the time the meat has cooked. Duck is one of those uncommon, common ingredients that's popping up in major grocery stores. The rich flavor of the breast is more like steak than poultry and it really holds up well to Asian flavors. Sweet roasted peaches provide contrast to the rich duck and spicy noodles.*

SERVES 4

2 ripe peaches, halved and pitted

Kosher salt and freshly ground black pepper

Extra-virgin olive oil

2 duck breasts (about 1¼ pounds total)

Toasted sesame oil

Cold Sesame Noodles (recipe follows)

Watercress, for garnish

Lime wedges, for garnish

Preheat the oven to 350°F. Sprinkle the peaches all over with salt and pepper. Put them cut sides up on a baking sheet and drizzle with olive oil. Throw them in the oven and roast until the peaches are very tender when you stick a knife in them, 15 to 20 minutes.

Meanwhile, put the duck breasts on a cutting board skin side up and score all over in a tiny crosshatch pattern so that as much of the fat as possible will render and the skin will crisp. Season all over with salt and pepper and drizzle with sesame oil. Film the bottom of a large sauté pan with olive oil and put the pan over medium heat. Add the breasts, skin side down, and cook slowly for about 10 minutes, until the fat is rendered and the skin is browned and crispy. Occasionally dump the fat out into a bowl. Turn the breasts and cook on the other side for 1 or 2 more minutes for medium-rare. Take the breasts out of the pan and put them on a platter to rest.

To serve, cut the duck breasts crosswise, on an angle, into 8 slices each. Mound the sesame noodles in 4 bowls. Add half of a sliced duck breast and a peach half to each bowl. Garnish with the watercress and lime wedges.

COLD SESAME NOODLES (SERVES 4)

Kosher salt

½ pound dried buckwheat (soba) noodles

9 tablespoons toasted sesame oil

1-inch piece of fresh ginger, peeled and smacked with the back of a knife

2 garlic cloves, smacked with the back of a knife

1 fresh red Thai chile or 1 jalapeño chile, minced, seeds and all

2 tablespoons brown sugar

½ cup creamy peanut butter

¼ cup rice vinegar

¼ cup low-sodium soy sauce

6 tablespoons hot water

1 tablespoon chile sauce or 1 teaspoon sambal

1 tablespoon sesame seeds, toasted

2 scallions, white and green parts, thinly sliced on the diagonal

Cook the soba noodles in a large pot of salted boiling water. Cook until barely tender and still firm, 3 to 4 minutes. Drain in a colander and rinse under cold running water to cool. Drain the noodles really well, transfer to a wide serving bowl, and toss immediately with 3 tablespoons of the sesame oil.

In a saucepan, heat 4 tablespoons of the sesame oil over medium-low heat. Add the ginger, garlic, and chile. Cook, stirring, for a minute until the vegetables are soft and fragrant. Dump that into a blender along with the brown sugar, peanut butter, vinegar, soy sauce, hot water, chile sauce, and the remaining 2 tablespoons of sesame oil; purée and refrigerate until cold.

Toss the noodles with the peanut sauce. Sprinkle with the sesame seeds and scallions.

CORNISH HENS WITH SOFT POLENTA, FENNEL SAUSAGE, AND RED GRAPES

IT SEEMS LIKE CORNISH HENS ARE THE NEW "IT" THING *at the poultry counter, and they're incredibly easy to cook. I like to stuff mine with rosemary and roast them in the oven until the skin is nice and crisp. If you're a sucker for traditional Tuscan food like I am, this dish will take you there like nothing else. The sweet fennel sausage and red wine cook down to a really silky sauce that wraps itself around the roasted hens.*

SERVES 4

4 (1- to 1½-pound) Cornish game hens

Kosher salt and freshly ground black pepper

2 tablespoons unsalted butter

POLENTA

1½ quarts chicken broth

¾ teaspoon kosher salt

1½ cups polenta or yellow cornmeal

¼ cup heavy cream

1½ tablespoons unsalted butter

¾ cup freshly grated Parmigiano-Reggiano cheese

1 teaspoon freshly ground black pepper

Extra-virgin olive oil

½ pound fresh fennel pork sausage, casings removed

2 tablespoons all-purpose flour

2 cups red wine

2 cups chicken broth

1½ cups halved red grapes

1 bunch of watercress, trimmed

Kosher salt and cracked black pepper

Preheat the oven to 400°F. Season the cavities of the hens with salt and pepper and tie the legs together with a piece of kitchen twine. Season all over with salt and pepper and put the hens in a single layer on a baking sheet. Put a dab of butter on top of each and roast for 45 to 50 minutes, until the skin is nice and crackly and an instant-read thermometer stuck into the thickest part of the thigh reads 160°F.

Meanwhile, make the polenta. First bring the chicken broth to a boil with the salt in a large saucepan. Then gradually pour in the cornmeal in a slow, steady stream, whisking constantly. Once the stock is completely absorbed, lower the heat and set a timer for 20 minutes. Continue cooking, whisking often, until the timer goes off; the polenta should be thick and smooth at this point. Then add the cream and butter and whisk for another 10 minutes. Stir in the cheese and pepper.

Meanwhile, make the sauce. Heat a 2-count of olive oil in a skillet over medium heat. Add the sausage and fry, stirring to break up the meat, for 3 or 4 minutes, until nice and brown. Dust with the flour and give it a stir to cook the flour. Then add the wine and broth, bring to a simmer, and let all that reduce for 5 to 7 minutes, until the mixture thickens to a saucy consistency.

To serve, toss the grape halves in a bowl with the watercress and a drizzle of olive oil; season with salt and cracked black pepper. Put a big spoonful of polenta on each plate and a hen on top. Spoon some of the sauce on the side. Garnish the plates with the watercress and grapes.

Warm, chewy noodles are a great way to put a smile on somebody's face; they're a blank canvas for a million flavor opportunities. Here's a collection of recipes that are drop-dead simple and span the calendar, from a quick summer pasta salad with the bright flavors of basil, blue cheese, and chicken, to the deep rootsy autumn flavors of mushrooms, smoky bacon, and caramelized cipolline onions and silky classics like spaghetti carbonara. One of my all-time favorite dishes—spaghetti with butter and Parmigiano—is so simple that you hardly need a recipe at all, but here you go: Cook a pound of spaghetti and drain it, reserving ¼ cup of the starchy cooking water. Throw that back in the pot, off the heat, with the spaghetti, ½ stick of cold butter, a cup of freshly grated Parmigiano-Reggiano and ¼ cup of extra-virgin olive oil; put the lid on and let it all melt for a few minutes. Stir it up and you've got a masterpiece.

HUNTERS' MINESTRONE

MINESTRONE IS A HEARTY ITALIAN VEGETABLE SOUP THAT
VARIES FROM REGION TO REGION. *Along the Riviera you'll
find a lighter and brothier soup made with tomato and lots of
fresh herbs; in northern Italy, toward Switzerland, it's made
with rice. This thick, soul-warming version with white beans,
pasta, aromatic vegetables, fresh pork sausage, olive oil, and
fresh sage is pulled from central Italy.*

SERVES 6, WITH LEFTOVERS

Kosher salt

10 cups chicken broth

8 garlic cloves, whacked with the side of a large knife, plus 3 cloves,
   chopped

¼ pound small rigatoni

Extra-virgin olive oil

8 fresh sage leaves

Needles from 1 fresh rosemary sprig

2 medium carrots, finely chopped

2 celery stalks, finely chopped

1 onion, finely chopped

¾ pound bulk pork sausage

1 can (28 ounces) plum tomatoes, drained and chopped

2 cans (28 ounces each) cannellini beans, drained

½ bunch of fresh flat-leaf parsley, chopped

1 bay leaf

Juice of ½ lemon

Coarsely ground black pepper

12 baguette slices

4 tablespoons (½ stick) unsalted butter, softened

1 cup freshly grated Parmigiano-Reggiano cheese

Bring a pot of salted water to a boil for the rigatoni.

Combine the broth and the smashed garlic cloves in a big
saucepan and simmer for about 15 minutes to give the stock a nice
garlicky taste; remove the garlic with a slotted spoon and discard.

Cook the rigatoni in the boiling water for 6 minutes; it should be
slightly underdone. Drain and set aside.

Meanwhile, pour ¼ cup olive oil into another big saucepan. Add
the sage and rosemary and warm the oil over medium heat to
infuse it with the flavor of the herbs, 3 to 4 minutes. Discard the
herbs. Add the carrots, celery, onion, and the chopped garlic and
cook for 3 to 4 minutes, until the vegetables are softened but not
browned. Dump that out onto a plate. Add a drizzle of oil to the pan,
then the sausage and cook, breaking up the sausage with the side
of a big spoon, until well browned. Return the vegetables to the pan
along with the drained tomatoes and cook for 5 minutes. Now add
the beans, parsley, bay leaf, lemon juice, broth, and lots of coarsely
ground black pepper. Bring to a simmer and cook for 15 minutes.
Stir in the cooked rigatoni. Discard the bay leaf.

To serve, preheat the broiler. Put the baguette slices in a single
layer on a baking sheet and brush with the softened butter. Sprinkle
with the Parmigiano and broil until the cheese is bubbly and golden
brown, about 3 minutes. Ladle the soup into bowls and float a
couple of croutons on top of each serving.

SUMMER BEEF NOODLE SALAD ·

THIS LIGHT, SUMMERTIME SALAD TRULY REPRESENTS THE AMERICAN PANTRY, *pulling inspiration from a few different cultures. The chewy rice noodles are Asian while the spicy, bright green dressing has a distinctive pesto-like consistency. Finished off with a few slices of New York strip and plump, roasted cherry tomatoes, the flavors are rich and simple. Add a cold glass of California chardonnay and you've got a new American classic.*

SERVES 4

Kosher salt

Extra-virgin olive oil

2 New York strip steaks (about 1½ pounds total),
   1¼ to 1½ inches thick

Freshly ground black pepper

1 pint cherry tomatoes

DRESSING

1½ bunches of arugula

Juice of 1 lime

¼ cup roasted peanuts

1 Thai bird chile

½ cup extra-virgin olive oil

Kosher salt

1 pound thin rice stick noodles (vermicelli)

1 bunch of arugula

Handful of fresh mint leaves

¼ cup roasted peanuts

Bring a big pot of salted water to a boil for the noodles.

Preheat the oven to 400°F. Put a large, ovenproof sauté pan over medium-high heat. Drizzle in a 2-count of olive oil and heat until the oil is smoking. Sprinkle the steaks all over with salt and pepper and sear in the hot pan for a couple of minutes on each side, until well browned. Shove the steaks to the side. Add the tomatoes to the pan, sprinkle with salt and pepper, drizzle with olive oil, and give them a stir to coat with the oil. Then put the pan in the oven and roast until the internal temperature of the beef reaches 125°F on an instant-read thermometer, 8 to 10 minutes. Remove the beef to a platter and let it rest for 10 minutes while you finish things up. Dump the tomatoes into a large bowl.

For the dressing, put the arugula, lime juice, peanuts, chile, and olive oil in a blender and purée. Season with salt.

Cook the rice noodles for 2 minutes in the boiling water until softened. Drain in a colander and add them to the bowl with the tomatoes. Add the lime dressing, the arugula, mint, and peanuts and give the whole thing a good toss. Cut the meat into thick slices and serve on top of the noodle salad.

THE ULTIMATE SPAGHETTI WITH CLAMS

I LIKE TO FINISH THIS DISH IN FRONT OF MY DINNER GUESTS *because when you pull the roasted clams with pancetta and tomatoes out of the oven, there's a big* WOW *factor. It's rustic, delicious, and dead simple and it might be one of the best pasta dishes I've ever made.*
  Serve with Herbed Garlic Bread (page 42).

SERVES 4

Kosher salt

40 littleneck clams

Extra-virgin olive oil

2 tablespoons unsalted butter

10 garlic cloves, smashed with the side of a knife

¼ pound pancetta, chopped

2 dried red chiles, crumbled, or ½ teaspoon crushed red pepper flakes

Handful of fresh basil leaves

¼ cup white wine

2 pints cherry tomatoes

Freshly ground black pepper

1 pound spaghetti

¼ cup chopped fresh flat-leaf parsley, for garnish

Preheat the oven to 400°F. Bring a big pot of salted water to a boil for the spaghetti.

Scrub the clams with a stiff brush under cold running water and discard any that are open. Put a medium roasting pan over two burners. Add a 2-count of olive oil, the butter, garlic, pancetta, chiles, and basil and cook until the pancetta renders its fat, 3 to 4 minutes. Add the clams, the wine, tomatoes, and a good amount of black pepper and toss that all together. Put the pan in the oven and roast until the clams open, about 10 minutes. (Discard any clams that do not open.)

Meanwhile, add the spaghetti to the boiling water and stir to keep the pasta from clumping together. Cook for 8 to 9 minutes, until al dente. Drain and put the spaghetti into a serving bowl; drizzle with olive oil and toss. Dump the clams and tomatoes with the cooking liquid over the spaghetti, add the parsley, and give it another toss.

THE ULTIMATE SPAGHETTI CARBONARA

SPAGHETTI CARBONARA WAS ONE OF THE FIRST AUTHENTIC PASTA DISHES I MASTERED *as a young line cook working in an Italian restaurant, and it's never lost its charm. The smoky bacon and silky egg sauce wrap around chewy strands of spaghetti; with lots of fresh cracked black pepper, it's so simple and delicious. In a silly way, it's like breakfast spaghetti.*

Another great thing about this dish is that eggs and bacon are inexpensive: If it weren't for spaghetti carbonara, I think I would have starved to death at college.

SERVES 4

Kosher salt

Extra-virgin olive oil

8 bacon slices, cut crosswise into thin strips

1 onion, chopped

4 large eggs

6 tablespoons heavy cream

¼ cup freshly grated Parmigiano-Reggiano cheese

1 pound spaghetti

Cracked black pepper

¼ cup chopped fresh flat-leaf parsley

Bring a big pot of salted water to a boil for the spaghetti.

Heat a 3-count of olive oil in a skillet over medium heat. Add the bacon and onion and cook for 7 to 8 minutes, until the onion is caramelized and the bacon is crisp. While that's going, crack the eggs into a big serving bowl. Add the cream and cheese and whisk. Scrape the bacon and onion into the bowl along with the cooking fat.

By now your pasta water has come to a boil. Throw in the spaghetti and give it a stir to separate the strands; cook for 8 to 9 minutes, until al dente. Scoop out about ¼ cup of the pasta cooking water and add that to the bowl with the bacon and eggs. Then drain the spaghetti, add it to the bowl, and give everything a toss. Invert a plate on top of the bowl to hold in the heat and let the pasta set for 5 minutes. Remove the plate, toss in some salt and lots of cracked black pepper and the parsley, and boom: You've got spaghetti carbonara!

BAKED RIGATONI WITH EGGPLANT AND PORK SAUSAGE

I LEARNED TO MAKE THIS DISH FROM THE LEGENDARY ANNA TASCA LANZA, *the Julia Child of Sicily. She has six books under her belt, a cooking school, and a family estate-run winery called Regaleali, so hanging out with her is a true lesson in southern Italian cooking.*

Anna shot an episode on eggplants with us for Tyler's Ultimate. In her family garden, she had more than ten varieties. She produced this amazing dish using eggplants that trace back to Tunisia. They were large, heart-shaped, and the color of purple midnight. She fried large cubes with lots of Sicilian extra-virgin olive oil, then tossed them with penne, garlicky homemade tomato purée, and pork sausage.

When I got back to New York, I made it with a few alterations: lots of creamy mozzarella cheese and a snow shower of Parmigiano-Reggiano. When you make this, not only will your house smell fantastic but you can truly taste the Sicilian countryside.

SERVES 6 TO 8

Kosher salt

Extra-virgin olive oil

4 links fennel pork sausage (about ³/₄ pound)

1 large eggplant (about 1¹/₂ pounds), cut into 1-inch pieces

1 large onion, chopped

3 garlic cloves, chopped

1 large can (28 ounces) peeled, whole tomatoes, preferably San Marzano

Leaves from 1 small bunch of basil

1 pound rigatoni

1 pound fresh mozzarella

Freshly ground black pepper

1 cup freshly grated Parmigiano-Reggiano cheese

Bring a large pot of salted water to a boil over high heat for the pasta. Get yourself a 9 by 13-inch Pyrex or ceramic baking dish.

Heat a 2-count of olive oil in a large skillet over medium-high heat. Add the sausages and toss in the hot oil for 3 to 4 minutes; you want them nicely browned on the outside but still rare inside. Put the sausages into the baking dish.

Turn the heat down to medium. Add a generous ¹/₃ cup of oil to the skillet and get it hot. Add as many eggplant pieces as you can comfortably fit in a single layer and sprinkle well with salt. Cook, turning, for 7 to 8 minutes, until the eggplant gets nice and browned, crisp on the outside, and soft inside. Use a spatula to put the eggplant into the baking dish with the sausage. Cook the rest of the eggplant pieces, adding more oil to the pan as needed and putting the finished eggplant into the baking dish.

Add another 2-count of oil to the skillet, then your onion and garlic, and cook for 3 to 4 minutes, until translucent. Dump the whole can of tomatoes and their juices into a bowl and crush the tomatoes with your hands to break them up; add that to the pan with the basil and cook it down until pulpy and relatively thick. This will take about 15 minutes.

By this time your pasta water will be boiling. Add the rigatoni, give it a stir, and cook for 6 to 7 minutes; it should still be slightly firm as it will cook further in the oven. Ladle out ¹/₂ cup of the pasta cooking water and reserve; then drain the rigatoni.

Preheat the oven to 450°F. Chop the sausages into nice big, bite-size chunky pieces and return the pieces to the baking dish. Add the tomato sauce, rigatoni, and the reserved pasta water. Break up half of the mozzarella over the mixture, season with salt and pepper, and gently mix that up with your hands or a spatula. Spread in an even layer and break the rest of the mozzarella over the top. Dust with the Parmigiano and drizzle with more olive oil. Bake for 25 minutes, or until golden and bubbling.

SPAGHETTI WITH SUMMER SQUASH AND TOMATOES

HERE'S AN AMAZING VEGETARIAN PASTA *that you can put together in the time it takes the pasta water to boil. Summer squash and cherry tomatoes are tossed with fresh oregano and extra-virgin olive oil and roasted on a sheet pan until they break down and get creamy; they cling to the spaghetti for dear life.*

I like a little peppery lettuce, such as arugula or watercress, to give the dish a spicy bite. Every time I make this pasta, I feel like I'm doing something good for myself.

SERVES 4

Kosher salt

1 zucchini, sliced into thin rounds

1 summer squash, sliced into thin rounds

1 pint cherry tomatoes

½ onion, finely chopped

1 garlic clove, chopped

1 tablespoon chopped fresh oregano

¼ cup extra-virgin olive oil

Freshly ground black pepper

1 pound spaghetti

Handful of arugula leaves

¾ cup freshly grated Parmigiano-Reggiano cheese, plus more for serving

Bring a large pot of salted water to a boil over high heat for the spaghetti.

Preheat the oven to 400°F. Combine the squashes, tomatoes, onion, garlic, and oregano in a large bowl. Add the olive oil, sprinkle with salt and pepper, and give it all a good toss. Dump that out onto a baking sheet and roast for 10 to 12 minutes, until the squash is tender and caramelized. Scrape the vegetables into a large pasta bowl and cover with a plate to keep everything warm.

Your pasta water should be boiling by now. Add the spaghetti and stir to separate the strands. Cook for 8 to 9 minutes, until al dente.

To finish, scoop out about ¼ cup of the pasta cooking water and add that to the bowl with the vegetables to keep them juicy. Drain the spaghetti and dump it into the bowl. Add the arugula and the Parmigiano and plenty of black pepper and toss. Taste for salt and serve with more Parmigiano.

TAGLIATELLE WITH MUSHROOMS, CIPOLLINE ONIONS, AND BACON

ONIONS AND BACON ARE GOD'S GIFT TO MUSHROOMS. *A special trick: This pasta is finished with a very simple Italian sauce called* burro fuso, *which is, very simply, starchy pasta water and butter cooked together and thickened with Parmigiano. Toss the whole thing with any fat ribbon noodle and you've got one of the best recipes in the book.*

SERVES 4

Kosher salt

Extra-virgin olive oil

¼ pound bacon, cut crosswise into thin strips

1 pint cipolline onions, peeled and halved

1 pound field mushrooms, or whatever mushrooms you find at the supermarket, such as shiitakes or creminis, sliced

2 garlic cloves, whacked with the side of a large knife

Needles from 1 small fresh rosemary sprig

Cracked black pepper

1 pound tagliatelle

4 tablespoons (½ stick) cold unsalted butter, cut into pieces

½ cup freshly grated Parmigiano-Reggiano cheese, plus extra for serving

Big handful of chopped fresh flat-leaf parsley

Bring a large pot of salted water to a boil over high heat for the pasta.

Heat a 3-count of olive oil in a large skillet over medium heat. Add the bacon and the onions and cook for 7 to 8 minutes to render the bacon fat and get the onions nice and browned. Add the mushrooms, garlic, and rosemary and cook for about 12 minutes, until the mushrooms are well caramelized. Season with salt and pepper and rake the vegetables out into a big serving bowl. Cover with a plate to keep warm. Don't wash the skillet; you'll need it for the sauce.

By now your pasta water should be at a boil; add the tagliatelle and get that cooking. Stir to separate the strands of pasta. Cook the pasta until al dente, 8 to 9 minutes. When the pasta is about halfway cooked, scoop out about 1 cup of the pasta water and add it to the skillet. Put the skillet over medium heat, add the cold butter, and simmer for 8 to 10 minutes, until the liquid is reduced and thickened to a nice sauce consistency.

Drain the tagliatelle and dump it into the bowl with the mushrooms and onions. Pour in the hot butter sauce. Add the Parmigiano, lots of cracked black pepper, and parsley. Give it a toss and you're done. Serve with more cheese.

SICILIAN-STYLE SPAGHETTI

I'VE HAD THIS SICILIAN CLASSIC AT A FEW NOTABLE ITALIAN RESTAURANTS *in New York, but I tasted the real deal while filming in Sicily. We broke for lunch at a trattoria in the capital city of Palermo. As soon as I saw* MACCHERONI CON LE SARDE—*pasta with fresh sardines, fennel, raisins, and pine nuts—on the menu, I snagged it.*

When I cooked it at home, I gave it a little twist by using one of my favorite flavors in the world—roasted cauliflower —and substituting anchovies for sardines. I'm not patting myself on the back but it's a noodle masterpiece and it only takes about a half hour.

SERVES 4

Kosher salt

1 head of cauliflower, cored and broken into small florets

Approximately ½ cup extra-virgin olive oil

2 anchovy fillets, mashed to a paste with the side of a large knife

¼ cup raisins

¼ cup toasted pine nuts

½ cup panko (Japanese bread crumbs)

Freshly ground black pepper

1 pound spaghetti

Leaves from ½ small bunch of fresh flat-leaf parsley, chopped

Juice of ½ lemon

Freshly grated Parmigiano-Reggiano cheese, for serving

Bring a big pot of salted water to a boil for the spaghetti.

Put the cauliflower into a sauté pan with ¼ cup olive oil and the anchovy fillets. Heat over medium heat until the oil is hot and the anchovy starts to sizzle. Add ¼ cup water and season with salt. Bring to a simmer over medium heat, cover, and steam the cauliflower for about 5 minutes until just tender; uncover and cook for an additional 5 to 7 minutes, until the water has evaporated and the cauliflower browns in the oil. Add the raisins and pine nuts and toss just to warm them through. Take the pan off the heat and cover with a lid to keep warm.

Meanwhile, preheat the oven to 350°F. On a baking sheet, drizzle the panko with 2 to 3 tablespoons olive oil and season with salt and pepper. Toss to coat the crumbs with the oil and spread out in an even layer; bake until lightly browned and crunchy, about 10 minutes. Set that aside.

When the water comes to a boil, get your spaghetti cooking; stir to separate the strands and cook for 8 to 9 minutes, until al dente.

You're almost finished now. Drain the spaghetti and dump it into a bowl. Add a 2-count of olive oil and toss. Dump the cauliflower mixture over the spaghetti, add the parsley and lemon juice, and fold it all together. To serve, use a pair of kitchen tongs to arrange a twist of pasta on each of 4 plates. Dust with the toasted panko and the cheese and serve.

FAT NOODLES WITH CRAB, BUTTERED ARTICHOKES, AND MINT

I SAVED SOME TIME WITH THIS DISH BY USING CANNED ARTICHOKES *and making them taste fantastic with a* burro fuso *(starchy pasta water, butter, and Parmigiano) that coats the artichokes with a thick, buttery glaze. I finish the dish with lemon zest, fresh crabmeat, and mint.*

SERVES 4

Kosher salt

1 pound pappardelle

4 tablespoons (½ stick) unsalted butter

½ cup extra-virgin olive oil

1 can (about 16 ounces) artichokes, drained, rinsed, and halved

Finely grated zest of ½ lemon

Pinch of crushed red pepper flakes

½ pint (8 ounces) lump crabmeat

Freshly ground black pepper

Handful of fresh mint leaves, chopped

¾ cup freshly grated Parmigiano-Reggiano cheese, plus extra for serving

Bring a large pot of salted water to a boil over high heat. Add the pappardelle, stir to separate, and cook for 8 to 9 minutes, until al dente. Drain and dump the pasta into a serving bowl. (You'll need to use 1 cup of the pasta cooking water for the sauce.)

While the pasta is cooking, combine the butter and olive oil in a medium skillet and put it over medium heat. Scoop out 1 cup of the pasta cooking water, add it to the skillet, and reduce the whole thing for 5 minutes to thicken. Then add the artichoke halves, lemon zest, red pepper flakes, crabmeat, and salt and pepper and toss to warm everything through. Add that to the bowl with the cooked, drained pasta. Add the mint and Parmigiano and season with salt and lots of black pepper. Toss and serve with extra Parmigiano.

THE ULTIMATE SPAGHETTI AND MEATBALLS

SPAGHETTI AND MEATBALLS CAN BE OUTSTANDING—OR VERY BORING; *it's the subtle nuances in the recipe that make all the difference. The meatballs should be tender enough to cut with a spoon but firm enough to hold together, and here's the trick: bread crumbs soaked in milk. It's a trick I picked up on in Naples, the meatball capital of the world. Without it, meatballs are chewy, like a well-done hamburger.*

SERVES 4 TO 6

Kosher salt

Extra-virgin olive oil

1 onion, chopped

2 garlic cloves, chopped

2 tablespoons finely chopped fresh flat-leaf parsley

1 cup milk

4 thick slices firm white bread, crusts removed, cut into cubes (about 2 cups)

1½ pounds ground beef

1½ pounds ground pork

1 large egg

½ cup freshly grated Parmigiano-Reggiano cheese, plus more for serving

Freshly ground black pepper

4 cups heated Pomodoro Sauce (recipe follows), or good-quality jarred tomato sauce

½ pound mozzarella cheese, grated

Leaves from 3 fresh basil sprigs

1 pound spaghetti

Bring a big pot of salted water to a boil for the spaghetti.

Heat 3 tablespoons of oil in an ovenproof skillet over medium heat. Add the onion, garlic, and parsley and cook until the vegetables are soft but not colored, about 10 minutes. Take the pan off the heat and let cool.

Pour the milk over the bread in a bowl and let it soak while the vegetables are cooling. Combine the meats in a large bowl. Add the egg and Parmigiano and season generously with salt and pepper. Use your hands to squeeze the excess milk out of the bread then add the bread to the bowl along with the cooled onion mixture. Gently combine all the ingredients with your hands until just mixed together; don't overwork. Shape the mixture into 10 meatballs.

Preheat the oven to 350°F. Heat a 3-count of oil in the skillet over medium heat and brown the meatballs on all sides, about 10 minutes. Transfer them to a baking dish and spoon about half of the tomato sauce over. Shower with the mozzarella and scatter half of the basil leaves on top; drizzle with olive oil. Put the meatballs in the oven and bake until they are cooked through, about 30 minutes.

Meanwhile, cook the spaghetti in the boiling water until al dente, 8 to 9 minutes. Drain the pasta and put it onto a large serving platter. Ladle on the rest of the sauce and toss. Spoon the meatballs onto the spaghetti and garnish with the rest of the basil leaves. Serve immediately along with extra cheese.

POMODORO SAUCE (MAKES 4 CUPS)

½ cup extra-virgin olive oil

1 medium onion, chopped

3 garlic cloves, chopped

2 cans (28 ounces each) whole, peeled tomatoes, preferably San Marzano, drained and crushed by hand, juices reserved

Kosher salt and freshly ground black pepper

¼ cup fresh basil leaves, torn into pieces

Heat the olive oil in a large saucepan over medium-low heat. Add the onion and garlic and cook until the vegetables are soft, 4 to 5 minutes. Carefully add the crushed tomatoes and about ½ cup of the reserved juices and season with salt and pepper. Cook until the sauce is thick, about 15 minutes. Taste and adjust the seasonings. Bring to a boil, stirring for a few minutes with a wooden spoon to further break up the tomatoes. Reduce the heat and let simmer for 20 to 30 minutes. Stir in the fresh basil and season again.

COLD PASTA SALAD WITH ROASTED CHICKEN, PLUMS, BLUE CHEESE, AND BASIL

I LOVE CHUNKY PASTA SALADS. *They're perfect for lunch or a simple early dinner and this recipe uses all my favorite ingredients. It all works: The roast chicken tastes great with the basil, and the blue cheese tastes great with the plums. Toss it all together with chewy cold pasta and you've got a big bowl of great stuff that'll be dinner tonight and a midnight snack tomorrow.*

You can save a step and make this with leftover roast chicken; roast the plums separately.

SERVES 4

Kosher salt

Extra-virgin olive oil

4 boneless, skinless chicken breasts

Freshly ground black pepper

1 pound plums, halved and pitted

1 pound penne

VINAIGRETTE

1 tablespoon Dijon mustard

1 teaspoon red wine vinegar

1 teaspoon sugar

⅓ cup extra-virgin olive oil

Kosher salt and freshly ground black pepper

1 bunch of fresh chives, minced

Handful of fresh flat-leaf parsley leaves, chopped

¼ pound crumbled blue cheese

Handful of whole fresh basil leaves

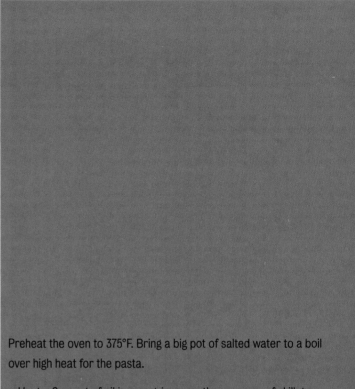

Preheat the oven to 375°F. Bring a big pot of salted water to a boil over high heat for the pasta.

Heat a 2-count of oil in a cast-iron or other ovenproof skillet over medium heat until almost smoking. Sprinkle the chicken breasts with a generous amount of salt and pepper and cook for 5 minutes, then flip the breasts and cook for 5 more minutes. Flip the breasts again, toss the pan in the oven, and roast for about 25 minutes, or until the juices run clear when you stick a small knife into the chicken. Meanwhile, toss the plums in a bowl with a drizzle of olive oil, salt, and pepper. Throw them in with the chicken during the last 8 minutes of cooking. Take the chicken and plums out of the pan, cool slightly, then stick them both in the refrigerator to chill.

Meanwhile, when the pasta water comes to a boil, add the penne and give it a stir to keep the penne from sticking together. Boil for 8 to 9 minutes, until al dente. Drain in a colander and chill under cold running water. Drain again.

The last thing is to make the vinaigrette: Whisk together the mustard, vinegar, and sugar in a large serving bowl. Whisk in the oil and season with salt and pepper. Fold in the herbs. Slice the chilled chicken and toss into the bowl along with the pasta, the blue cheese, and the basil leaves. Toss, and taste for seasoning. Mound on a plate with the plums alongside.

THE ULTIMATE MACARONI AND CHEESE WITH PEAS AND BACON

I DON'T KNOW A MAN, WOMAN, OR CHILD WHO DOESN'T LOVE A BOWL OF GREAT MAC AND CHEESE. *Sweet peas and bacon spooned on top take it to a whole new level. This is the one and only macaroni and cheese recipe you will ever need.*

SERVES 6 TO 8

Kosher salt

1 pound elbow macaroni

3 tablespoons unsalted butter

3 tablespoons all-purpose flour

4 cups warm milk

5½ cups shredded sharp white Cheddar cheese

Freshly ground black pepper

¼ cup chopped fresh flat-leaf parsley

Extra-virgin olive oil

4 slices bacon, cut crosswise into thin strips

1 large onion, diced

2 garlic cloves, smashed

Leaves from ¼ bunch of fresh thyme

2 cups frozen peas, thawed in a colander under cool water

Bring a pot of salted water to a boil over high heat. Add the macaroni and cook for 8 to 9 minutes, until al dente. Drain.

Preheat the oven to 400°F.

Melt the butter in a large, deep skillet over medium heat. Whisk in the flour and cook for about 1 minute, stirring constantly to keep lumps from forming. Gradually whisk in the milk and, whisking vigorously, cook until the mixture is thick and smooth. Stir in 4 cups of the cheese and continue to cook and stir to melt the cheese. Season with salt and pepper. Add the cooked macaroni and the parsley and fold that all in to coat the macaroni with the cheese mixture. Scrape into a 3-quart baking dish and sprinkle with the remaining 1½ cups cheese. Bake for 30 minutes, or until hot and bubbly.

While that's going, heat a 2-count of olive oil in a sauté pan. Add the bacon, onion, garlic, and thyme and cook for about 5 minutes to soften the onion. Fold in the peas and season with salt and pepper.

To serve, scatter the pea and bacon mixture over the mac and cheese. Use a big spoon to scoop out servings, making sure you get some of the smoky pea mixture on each spoonful.

Just to prove how important vegetables are, let me offer two simple illustrations of seasonality. Take a dish of chicken breast marinated in extra-virgin olive oil and lemon juice and then grilled. In the summer, I'd serve that with tomatoes, fresh cucumber, black olives, and salad greens: fresh, bright, crisp. For a completely different effect in the winter I'd replace the summer vegetables with roasted Brussels sprouts, apples, sage, and smoked bacon; now the effect is hearty and warming. Same chicken breast, two completely different meals. This example proves that not only are vegetables the barometer of the season, they're also the missing piece of the puzzle that truly determines the meal. I really love cooking with fresh vegetables. At the end of the day, a chicken breast is just a chicken breast but with a careful trip to the produce section, you can take it in an amazing number of different directions. Here's a chapter full of well-thought-out recipes that will save you some time in the kitchen and also give your cooking tons of personality, season after season.

THE ULTIMATE SALAD: GREEN, YELLOW, OR RED

WHEN IT COMES TO VEGETABLES, PEOPLE EAT WITH THEIR EYES. *Here are three ultimate salads broken down by color —green, yellow, and red—using all of your favorite ingredients. They will quickly become your go-to salads for a weeknight side dish or an excellent course for a dinner party.*

And here's the kicker: I've got one ultimate homemade salad dressing that's amazing with all three.

MAKES ABOUT ⅓ CUP
ULTIMATE VINAIGRETTE
1 shallot, finely minced
1 teaspoon Dijon mustard
2 teaspoons red wine vinegar
¼ cup extra-virgin olive oil
1 teaspoon sugar
1 teaspoon honey
Kosher salt and freshly ground black pepper

Combine the shallot, mustard, vinegar, oil, sugar, honey, and salt and pepper in a jar and shake to emulsify.

GREEN SALAD (SERVES 4)
6 cups mixed arugula, mâche, and Bibb lettuces
1 cup green grapes
¼ cup pistachios
Handful of fresh dill sprigs
1 recipe Ultimate Vinaigrette (at left)

Combine the lettuces, grapes, pistachios, and dill in a bowl. Pour the vinaigrette over all and toss.

YELLOW SALAD (SERVES 4)
Kosher salt
½ pound yellow wax beans, trimmed
2 heads of frisée (hearts only), broken apart by hand
2 heads of Belgian endive, bases trimmed, and leaves separated
½ cup yellow teardrop tomatoes, halved
2 tablespoons toasted pine nuts
1 recipe Ultimate Vinaigrette (at left)

Bring a large pot of salted water to a boil. Fill a large bowl with ice water and add salt to it until it tastes lightly salty. When the water comes to a boil, add the beans and cook until just tender, about 3 minutes. Drain, then refresh in the water bath; drain again.

Combine the beans, frisée, endive, tomatoes, and pine nuts in a bowl. Pour the vinaigrette over all and toss.

RED SALAD (SERVES 4)
6 cups mixed radicchio and red leaf lettuces
1 red Bartlett pear, halved, cored but not peeled, and thinly sliced
¼ cup toasted walnut halves
1 recipe Ultimate Vinaigrette (at left)

Combine the lettuces, pear, and walnuts in a bowl. Pour the vinaigrette over all and toss.

GREEN BEAN SALAD WITH BLACK OLIVE AND CREME FRAICHE DRESSING

FRESH, CRUNCHY GREEN BEANS TASTE LIKE A TALL, REFRESHING GLASS OF WATER. *With this recipe, I've turned green beans into an excellent side dish with a creamy dressing, a hint of lemon, and salty black olives. You've got a simple, sophisticated dish that'll taste amazing with anything off the grill.*

SERVES 4

Kosher salt

1 pound green beans, trimmed

1 cup crème fraîche

Juice of 1 lemon

¼ cup extra-virgin olive oil

Freshly ground black pepper

¼ cup pitted kalamata olives

Fresh dill sprigs, for garnish

Bring a large pot of salted water to a boil. Fill a large bowl with ice water and add salt to it until it tastes lightly salty. When the water comes to a boil, add the beans and cook until just tender, about 3 minutes. Drain, then refresh in the water bath to keep the bright green color, and drain well again. Put the beans in a bowl.

In a blender, combine the crème fraîche, lemon juice, olive oil, and salt and pepper to taste and blend until smooth. Pour over the green beans. Add the olives and toss. Garnish with dill sprigs.

THE ULTIMATE COLESLAW WITH PECANS AND SPICY CHILE DRESSING

COLESLAW IS SUCH AN EASY DISH TO GET RIGHT. *With this recipe, it's even easier to make it taste delicious! I'm a big fan of lots of crunchy texture, provided here by sweet apples and pecans. The creamy dressing has a bold kick from a couple of dashes of cayenne and cumin, and a handful of mint at the end gives it an unexpected, fresh flavor.*

SERVES 6 TO 8

1 head napa or Savoy cabbage, shredded

4 carrots, shredded

2 Granny Smith apples, cored but not peeled, and thinly sliced

1 medium red onion, thinly sliced

1 cup pecans, toasted and chopped

DRESSING

1 tablespoon Dijon mustard

1 teaspoon sugar

½ teaspoon cayenne

½ teaspoon ground cumin

¾ cup mayonnaise

Juice of 1 lemon

Kosher salt and freshly ground black pepper

Leaves from 1 bunch of fresh mint, for garnish

Throw the cabbage, carrots, apples, onion, and pecans into a large bowl. Mix that well with your hands and set aside.

In a small bowl, stir together the mustard, sugar, cayenne, cumin, mayonnaise, and lemon juice until blended. Season with salt and pepper. Pour the dressing over the cabbage mixture and toss well to coat. Taste again for seasoning, then mound onto a platter and garnish with mint leaves.

TOLAN'S MOM'S POTATO SALAD

SOMETIMES YOU HAVE TO GIVE CREDIT WHERE CREDIT IS DUE. *This recipe belongs to Marge Clark from Marin County, California, and she knows who she is. I thought I knew potato salad until I tasted this. It's the best potato salad I've ever made, I swear.*

SERVES 4 TO 6

2 pounds small Yukon Gold potatoes

2 large eggs

Kosher salt

½ bunch of sliced scallions, white and green parts

2 tablespoons drained capers

1 cup mayonnaise

¼ cup Dijon mustard

¼ cup finely chopped dill pickles with ¼ cup juice

1 small red onion, chopped

2 tablespoons chopped fresh flat-leaf parsley

Juice of ½ lemon

Freshly ground black pepper

Extra-virgin olive oil, for drizzling

Put the potatoes and eggs into a big saucepan of cold, salted water. (Cooking the potatoes with the skin on keeps in their natural flavor so they taste amazing.) Bring to a simmer. After 12 minutes remove the eggs with a slotted spoon and let cool. Continue cooking the potatoes until a paring knife poked into them goes in without resistance, about 3 minutes longer. Drain the potatoes in a colander and let them cool.

Reserve some scallion greens and capers for garnish. Meanwhile, stir together the mayonnaise, mustard, pickles with juice, onion, remaining scallions and capers, parsley, and lemon juice in a bowl large enough to hold the potatoes. Peel the cooled eggs and grate them into the bowl. Stick a fork into the potatoes, one at a time, lift them out of the colander, and peel with a paring knife. Break up the potatoes into rough chunks by hand right into the bowl and toss to coat with the dressing. Season to taste with salt and pepper. Garnish with the reserved scallions and capers. Drizzle with a little olive oil before serving.

THE ULTIMATE BAKED BEANS

BAKED BEANS ARE AN INSTITUTION OF THE AMERICAN PICNIC. *This dish has all the sweet barbecued flavors you've come to expect but with a spicy punch from chipotle chiles. The dressing is super easy—the whole thing happens in a blender—and because it's made with canned beans the dish comes together in a fraction of the time you might think.*

Before it goes in the oven, I top the dish off with thick slabs of smoky bacon and the needles from a few sprigs of fresh rosemary. It's the right side dish for any outdoor barbecue and the whole thing takes only half an hour.

SERVES 6

½ cup molasses

¼ cup ketchup

2 tablespoons Dijon mustard

2 canned chipotle chiles in adobo

3 big (28-ounce) cans cannellini beans

Kosher salt and freshly ground black pepper

10 bacon strips

3 to 4 fresh rosemary sprigs

Preheat the oven to 350°F. Put the molasses, ketchup, mustard, and chiles in a blender and purée. Scrape that into a big bowl, add the beans, season with salt and black pepper, and gently toss so that the beans are coated with the molasses mixture. Now dump that into a 9 by 13-inch baking dish and level it. Shingle the bacon strips over the top. Throw the rosemary sprig on top and bake until the bacon is browned and fat is rendered, about 25 minutes.

ROASTED ROOT VEGETABLES WITH HONEY, BALSAMIC VINEGAR, AND FRESH GOAT CHEESE

IN THE FALL, MY FAVORITE VEGETABLES ARE SIMPLE ROOTS . . . ROASTED. *And the vinaigrette in this dish is absolutely delicious; the honey and the balsamic come together as if they've known each other for years.*

SERVES 4

½ pound medium carrots, peeled and left whole

½ pound medium beets, peeled and quartered

½ pound medium turnips, peeled and halved

½ pound medium parsnips, peeled and left whole

3 shallots, unpeeled, cut in half through the stem end

¼ cup extra-virgin olive oil

Kosher salt and freshly ground black pepper

¼ cup honey

¼ cup balsamic vinegar

4 ounces chilled fresh goat cheese

Preheat the oven to 350°F. Toss the vegetables with the olive oil and salt and pepper in a big bowl. Dump them out onto a baking sheet in a single layer and roast for 25 minutes. Whisk together the honey and vinegar in a small bowl. Take the vegetables out of the oven, pour the vinegar-honey mixture over, and toss. Return the vegetables to the oven and cook until fork-tender and caramelized, about 20 more minutes. Top with pieces of goat cheese and that's it.

BORLOTTI BEANS
WITH WOODY HERBS

TUSCAN-STYLE BORLOTTI BEANS ARE NOTHING MORE THAN PEASANT FOOD, REFINED FOR HIGH ART. *This simple dish can be taken in so many different directions: served with chunks of fresh sausage as a hearty soup, as a side dish with steak or roasted chicken, or thinned with a couple of cups of vegetable stock for a hearty vegetarian soup. The Old World process takes a few hours but I have cut the time by fortifying canned beans with carrot, celery, onion, and sage.*

SERVES 4 TO 6

1 onion, quartered

1 carrot, cut into large chunks

1 celery stalk

3 garlic cloves

3/4 cup extra-virgin olive oil

4 fresh thyme sprigs

2 fresh sage sprigs

1 small fresh rosemary sprig

1/2 teaspoon crushed red pepper flakes

2 cans (28 ounces each) borlotti beans

2 bay leaves

2 cups chicken broth

Kosher salt and freshly ground black pepper

Put the onion, carrot, celery, and garlic in a food processor and pulse to chop fine. Heat 1/4 cup of the olive oil in a large pot over medium heat. Add the herbs and cook for 1 to 2 minutes. Add the finely chopped vegetables and red pepper flakes and sauté until the vegetables are soft, about 3 minutes. Add the beans, bay leaves, broth, and remaining 1/2 cup of olive oil. Bring to a boil, reduce the heat, and simmer, partially covered, for 20 minutes, or until the beans are flavorful. Taste for salt and pepper. Discard the bay leaves before serving the beans.

VELVET POTATO PURÉE

I'VE BEEN COOKING FOR A LONG TIME *and if there's one thing I know how to cook really well, it's mashed potatoes. Mine are smooth and extra-rich, like a coat of warm velvet across your tongue.*

The secret to making delicious potatoes is a simple tool called a ricer. Once the potatoes are cooked, the ricer breaks them down to a dry, snowy powder that you reconstitute with cream and butter. This potato purée is excellent served with everything from scallops to sautéed pork chops with apples, or even just with a big spoon.

———————

SERVES 4

3 large Yukon Gold potatoes, peeled and quartered

Kosher salt

1 cup heavy cream

4 tablespoons (½ stick) unsalted butter

Freshly ground black pepper

Extra-virgin olive oil

Put the potatoes in a medium saucepan with cold water to cover. Add 1 teaspoon salt, bring to a boil, reduce the heat, and simmer for 15 to 20 minutes, until the potatoes are very tender. While they cook, warm the cream with the butter in a small saucepan over medium heat until the butter melts. Drain the potatoes and pass them through a food mill or a ricer into a large mixing bowl. Stir in the warm cream and butter until the liquid is absorbed and the mixture is smooth. Season with salt and pepper and stir in a drizzle of olive oil.

ASPARAGUS STEAMED IN A PAPER BAG

I BUY ASPARAGUS AT THE GROCERY STORE JUST LIKE EVERY-
ONE ELSE *and yes, there are a million ways to cook it. But
this recipe is the easiest way I know to really maximize its
flavor.*

*When you blanch asparagus, a lot of the nutrients and
flavor get leached out into the water, leaving the asparagus
relatively bland tasting. But when it's steamed in the oven in
a small container like a paper bag with extra-virgin olive oil,
thinly sliced lemon, and a bay leaf to season it, the flavor
explodes. After it's been in the oven for 20 minutes, I take the
brown bag to the table and give it two shakes, and the
asparagus falls out. It's bright green and perfectly steamed
with an incredibly fresh flavor.*

SERVES 4

1 pound medium asparagus, tough ends trimmed

Extra-virgin olive oil

Sea salt and cracked black pepper

½ lemon, sliced paper-thin

1 bay leaf

Preheat the oven to 350°F and arrange an oven rack in the middle of the oven. Get yourself a paper bag large enough to hold the asparagus comfortably. Throw the asparagus in there and drizzle the outside of the bag with olive oil to keep the bag from burning. Sprinkle the asparagus with salt and cracked pepper and toss in the lemon slices and bay leaf. Close the bag, folding it over several times and creasing the folds well to hold the steam in. Put the bag on a baking sheet, drizzle it with more olive oil, stick it in the oven, and bake for 20 minutes.

Take the baking sheet out of the oven and set it on top of the stove. Set a serving plate next to the stove. Using a kitchen towel or a pair of tongs, raise the bag over the plate, open the bag, and slide the asparagus out onto the plate. Drizzle with a little more olive oil and serve hot.

GRILLED EGGPLANT WITH LEMON, YOGURT, POMEGRANATE, AND MINT

WHEN YOU PREPARE EGGPLANT, SCORING THE FLESH OPENS UP THE SURFACE AREA SO THAT IT COOKS MORE QUICKLY. *I love eggplant simply tossed in extra-virgin olive oil and grilled until the outside gets charred and the inside is creamy soft. And because eggplant has such a neutral flavor, it goes with anything. You can sauce it with a pesto, a tomato sauce, or a combination of soy sauce, brown sugar, and rice wine vinegar. I particularly like it with Middle Eastern flavors.*

SERVES 4

8 small (4-inch-long) eggplants, trimmed, split in half, flesh scored
Extra-virgin olive oil
Kosher salt and freshly ground black pepper

1 cup plain yogurt
2 tablespoons tahini or smooth peanut butter
Juice of 1 lemon
2 teaspoons ground cumin
Handful of fresh mint leaves
1 pomegranate, cracked open and seeds dug out
1 red Thai chile, sliced

Put a large grill pan on two burners over medium-high heat or preheat an outdoor gas or charcoal grill to medium. If you're using an outdoor grill, take a few paper towels and fold them over several times to make a thick square. Blot a small amount of oil on the paper towel, then carefully and quickly wipe the hot grates of the grill to make a nonstick grilling surface.

Put the eggplant halves on a big platter or sheet pan. Drizzle with olive oil and sprinkle on both sides with salt and pepper. Put the eggplant slices on the grill and cook until golden, 4 to 5 minutes. Then turn and continue cooking for 4 to 5 minutes more, until nicely browned on both sides and soft and creamy.

Meanwhile, put the yogurt, tahini, lemon juice, 2 tablespoons olive oil, the cumin, and salt and pepper into a blender and purée until smooth. Taste for salt and pepper.

To serve, spread the yogurt sauce over the bottom of a serving platter. Shingle the eggplant halves on top and garnish with the mint, pomegranate seeds, and sliced chile.

THE ULTIMATE SPINACH SALAD WITH BACON, BLACK PEPPER, AND HONEY

NOTHING FEELS BETTER WHEN I'M SHOPPING THAN KNOW-ING THAT I CAN GRAB A BAG OF FRESH BABY SPINACH AND HAVE DINNER ON THE TABLE IN TWENTY MINUTES. *This is a perfect entrée-size salad for any night of the week. Sweet honey and vinegar are cooked down until nice and thick, then I toss with fresh spinach and crispy bacon. I love this salad with eggs and lots of black pepper.*

SERVES 4

2 large eggs

2 bacon slices, cut crosswise into thin strips

1 onion, sliced

2 garlic cloves, whacked with the side of a chef's knife so that they fall into big pieces

2 tablespoons honey

1 tablespoon apple cider vinegar

1 bag (1 pound) baby spinach

Kosher salt and freshly ground black pepper

Put the eggs in a small saucepan and cover with cold water. Bring to a simmer over medium-high heat, turn the heat off and let the eggs sit for 12 minutes. Lift the eggs out of the pan and cool; peel the eggs.

Meanwhile, put the bacon strips into a big skillet and cook for 3 to 4 minutes over medium heat to render the fat. Scoop the bacon out and set it aside on a plate, leaving the fat in the pan. Add the onion and garlic and cook for 5 to 6 minutes, until soft. Add the honey and vinegar and keep cooking until the onion has caramelized, about 5 more minutes. Toss the spinach into the pan, sprinkle with salt and pepper, and toss with tongs until the spinach is just wilted, about 30 seconds. Dump the spinach out into a bowl and add the bacon. Halve the eggs and arrange atop the salad.

ROASTED BROCCOLI WITH CRISPY PARMESAN AND LEMON

LET'S FACE IT, BROCCOLI DOESN'T HAVE A LOT OF SEX APPEAL. *It usually shows up steamed, or in a casserole with Ritz crackers on top, or condensed in a can of soup. Roasting is my favorite way to cook vegetables; since broccoli is a little thick, it needs to be blanched for a few minutes first. Then it goes in a baking pan where it's dusted with a snow shower of Parmigiano cheese and popped in the oven. The broccoli caramelizes on the bottom of the pan as it roasts and the Parmigiano melts and becomes quite crunchy and nutty tasting. It's even better with the squeeze of fresh lemon.*

SERVES 4

Kosher salt

2 heads of broccoli (about 3 pounds)

1 cup freshly grated Parmigiano-Reggiano cheese

Juice of 1 lemon

Preheat the oven to 400°F and bring a big pot of salted water to a boil. Trim about 1 inch off the ends of the broccoli stalks and peel the stalks with a vegetable peeler. Cut the broccoli lengthwise into spears. When the water comes to a boil, add the broccoli and cook for 3½ minutes, until the broccoli is just tender and still bright green. Drain in a colander. Arrange the broccoli in a nonstick ovenproof pan. Sprinkle the cheese evenly over the top and bake until the cheese melts and forms a crisp shell over the broccoli, about 10 minutes. Lift the broccoli out onto a platter with a spatula and hit it with a squeeze of fresh lemon.

THE ULTIMATE RATATOUILLE

IN THE SUMMER I MAKE A BIG BATCH OF RATATOUILLE ONCE A WEEK *and leave it in the fridge to snack on all week. It's delicious tossed with pasta or served chilled as an appetizer with soft goat cheese and crunchy bread. Best-case scenario, give this a few hours to rest before you eat it so the flavors come together like they do in a good soup.*

_____

SERVES 4

⅓ cup plus ½ cup extra-virgin olive oil

1 pound smallish Italian eggplants, cut into 1-inch cubes

Kosher salt and freshly ground black pepper

1 pound zucchini, cut crosswise into 1-inch sections

3 anchovy fillets, finely minced

2 onions, finely chopped

3 garlic cloves, finely chopped

¼ cup chopped fresh flat-leaf parsley

Leaves from ½ bunch of fresh basil, coarsely chopped

Leaves from 4 fresh thyme sprigs

2 pints cherry tomatoes

1 dried chile

Splash of balsamic vinegar

Line a large platter with paper towels. Heat ⅓ cup olive oil in a medium saucepan over medium heat. Add the eggplant, season generously with salt and pepper, and let that cook down for 10 to 12 minutes, until the eggplant is nice and soft and wilted. Move the eggplant out of the pan and onto the platter to drain. Next stop, zucchini: Cook it the same way in ¼ cup oil, then add it to the platter with the eggplant.

Add another ¼ cup olive oil to the pan, then the anchovies, onions, garlic, and herbs. Cook for 5 to 7 minutes, until the onions get nice and caramelized. Add the tomatoes and cook that down for 10 to 12 minutes, until pulpy. Return the eggplant and zucchini to the pan, crack open the chile, and add that, too. Season with salt and pepper and let the ratatouille cook slowly for about 20 minutes, until the mixture is soft, mushy, and juicy; you want all the flavors to come together. Stir in the vinegar and let cool to room temperature.

OVEN FRIES

CRISPY OVEN FRIES ARE A GREAT WAY TO GET THAT CLASSIC BISTRO EFFECT *without having to heat up a pot of oil. The wedges are tossed in a healthy amount of extra-virgin olive oil and roasted in the oven until very crisp.*

There are two tricks to making these. Roast at a high temperature, and don't shake the fries around while they're cooking; the longer they sit in contact with the metal baking sheet, the crisper they get. Tossed with chopped parsley and freshly grated Parmigiano, they'll make any French-fry lover happy.

SERVES 4

2 russet potatoes, cut in half lengthwise, halves cut lengthwise into fourths to make 16 big, fat wedges

¼ cup extra-virgin olive oil

¾ teaspoon kosher salt

¼ cup freshly grated Parmigiano-Reggiano cheese

2 tablespoons chopped fresh flat-leaf parsley

Preheat the oven to 425°F. Toss the potatoes with the olive oil and salt in a large bowl, then dump the potatoes out onto a baking sheet, spreading to a single layer. Roast for 30 to 35 minutes, until the potatoes are cooked through, brown, and crispy. Toss them in a big bowl with the cheese and parsley and serve hot.

ROASTED DUMPLING SQUASH

I HADN'T PLANNED TO INCLUDE THIS PARTICULAR RECIPE *but there were a few of these dumpling squash at the photo shoot the day we shot this chapter and they looked so great I made up this recipe on the fly. It uses a few simple things I had in my cabinet: brown sugar, butter, amaretto, and sage. The flavorings seep into the squash as it roasts and becomes as soft as pudding. This is a perfect vegetable dish for any time in the fall, especially Thanksgiving.*

SERVES 4

2 dumpling squash, about 1 pound each

Kosher salt and freshly ground black pepper

½ cup (1 stick) unsalted butter, softened

½ cup brown sugar

3 tablespoons amaretto liqueur

8 fresh sage leaves

½ pound crushed pignoli cookies (from your local Italian bakery), or amaretti cookies

Preheat the oven to 350°F. Split the squash in half through the equators and scrape out the seeds with a spoon. Set the squash halves, cut sides up, on a baking sheet and sprinkle with salt and pepper.

In a bowl, cream the butter with the brown sugar and amaretto. Brush the cut sides of each squash half with the butter mixture and put 2 sage leaves on top of each. Sprinkle with the crushed cookies. Bake until tender, 30 to 35 minutes, basting every 15 minutes with some of the butter that has pooled in the center.

I always approach desserts from a cook's point of view. The flavors have to be simple, delicious, and to the point without taking all afternoon. I love gooey, sensational desserts that taste complex but are really effortless. This chapter's full of recipes that will blow away most desserts you can find at a restaurant, and only you and I will know how truly easy they are to make.

THE ULTIMATE BERRY TRIFLE

THIS IS A SHOWSTOPPING DESSERT THAT PRACTICALLY MAKES ITSELF. *When you can buy perfectly good lemon curd and pound cake at the grocery store, there's no point in making them yourself. The berries are cooked very quickly with lemon juice and sugar to pull out their natural flavors and the lemon curd is lightened with freshly whipped cream. The total effect is a terrific dessert that takes about half an hour to put together—and people go nuts over it.*

SERVES 4

BERRIES

1 pint blueberries

1 pint strawberries, hulled and cut into thick slices

1 pint raspberries

¼ cup sugar

1½ teaspoons cornstarch

Juice of 1 lemon

LEMON CREAM

1 cup heavy cream

1 tablespoon sugar

½ teaspoon vanilla extract

1 cup store-bought lemon curd

1 store-bought pound cake, sliced ½ inch thick

Combine the berries, sugar, cornstarch, and lemon juice in a saucepan over medium-high heat. Bring to a simmer and cook just until the berries begin to break down and give up their juices, about 3 minutes. Take the berries off the heat and let cool; the mixture should thicken up as it cools.

In a clean bowl, whip the cream with the sugar and vanilla to soft peaks. Put the lemon curd into a second bowl and stir in a little of the whipped cream to loosen it. Then fold in the rest of the cream.

To assemble the trifle, spoon a layer of the lemon cream into a large glass bowl. Add a layer of pound cake, breaking the slices into pieces to fit. Then soak the cake with a layer of berries and their juices. Keep going to make 3 or 4 more layers, depending on the size of the bowl, finishing with a layer of lemon cream. Cover and refrigerate until ready to serve.

PEAR COBBLER WITH CRANBERRY STREUSEL

THE WARM, MELTED FRUIT COMBINATION OF PEARS AND CRANBERRIES MAKES A FANTASTIC COMFORT-FOOD DESSERT *to warm up even the coldest night. Grab a bowlful with a scoop of ice cream and slip on a thick pair of socks: You've got the ultimate winter nightcap.*

SERVES 4

Unsalted butter, at room temperature

Granulated sugar

4 Bartlett pears

2 teaspoons vanilla extract

¼ cup brown sugar

2 tablespoons all-purpose flour

1 teaspoon cinnamon

½ teaspoon ground nutmeg

STREUSEL TOPPING

½ cup (1 stick) unsalted butter, softened

½ cup brown sugar

½ cup all-purpose flour

½ teaspoon kosher salt

1 cup fresh or frozen cranberries

½ cup heavy cream, beaten to soft peaks

Preheat the oven to 350°F. Butter an 8 by 8-inch baking dish. Dust the dish with granulated sugar, tapping out any excess.

Peel the pears and cut them in half through the stem end. Use a melon baller to scoop out the cores. Put the pear halves in a large bowl, sprinkle with the vanilla, and toss. Then sprinkle over the brown sugar, flour, cinnamon, and nutmeg and toss so that the pears are really well coated with the flavorings. Set the pears in a single layer, cored side down, in the prepared baking dish.

Now make the topping. In the same bowl, combine the butter, brown sugar, flour, and salt and mash it all together with your fingers. Toss in the cranberries. Crumble the topping mixture over the pears in the baking dish and bake until the topping is nice and crunchy and browned and the pears are very tender, 35 to 40 minutes. Serve with whipped cream.

LEMON RICOTTA CREPES WITH BLUEBERRIES AND FRESH BANANAS

THIS RECIPE, AKA THE BLINTZ, WILL KNOCK YOUR SOCKS OFF. *Although it requires a little more patience than some of the other recipes in this chapter, the result is chic, simple, and sophisticated. If you've never made crepes before, the good news is that with a few pushes of a button, the recipe comes together in a blender in a few minutes. The bad news is that it might take you a crepe or two until you get the hang of cooking them. The trick is to roll the pan so that the bottom gets evenly and very thinly coated with the batter for ultra-thin pancakes. But don't worry, this recipe makes enough batter so that you can toss a few of the misfires and still have enough crepes for the recipe.*

SERVES 4

CREPES

1⅓ cups all-purpose flour

1 large pinch of salt

1¾ cups milk

2 large eggs

10 tablespoons (1¼ sticks) unsalted butter, melted, plus more melted butter for the pans

FILLING

1 container (15 ounces) ricotta cheese

Finely grated zest of 1 lemon

¼ cup confectioners' sugar

1 large egg

BLUEBERRY SAUCE

2 tablespoons unsalted butter

2 pints blueberries

¾ cup granulated sugar

1 teaspoon cornstarch

Juice of 1 lemon

2 ripe bananas, quartered

In a blender, combine the flour, salt, milk, and eggs and blend on medium speed until the batter is smooth. Pour in the melted butter and blend just for a second to incorporate it. The batter should be smooth and shiny. Pour it through a fine sieve into a bowl to get rid of any lumps and refrigerate for 1 hour.

Put an 8-inch crepe pan or a nonstick skillet over medium heat and brush with a little melted butter. Pour about ¼ cup of the batter into the pan (a 2-ounce ladle works well for this) and swirl it around so that the batter just covers the bottom of the pan; pour any excess batter back into the bowl. (A good crepe should be paper-thin.) Cook for 30 to 45 seconds, until the batter just sets and you see the edge turning golden brown. Flip the crepe and cook for another 30 seconds to brown the other side. Slide the crepe off onto a plate, put the pan back on the heat, and keep making crepes until all of the batter is used. Cover the crepes with a clean kitchen towel or plastic wrap to keep them from drying out while you work.

For the filling, stir together the ricotta, lemon zest, confectioners' sugar, and egg in a bowl.

Now you're ready to put these babies together. Preheat the oven to 400°F. Put a crepe on a cutting board in front of you, the best-looking side facing down. Spoon about ¼ cup of the cheese filling along the lower third of the crepe. Fold the bottom edge up to just cover the filling, then fold the 2 sides into the center. Roll the crepe over and away from you to make a package, seam side down. Continue to fill and roll 8 crepes.

Add a little melted butter to a medium skillet over medium heat. Put half of the filled crepes in the pan and cook for 2 minutes on each side, or until crisp and golden. Transfer to a baking dish. Brown the rest of the crepes the same way, put them into the baking dish, and then put that into the oven. Bake for 10 minutes to firm the filling.

While the crepes are in the oven, combine all the blueberry sauce ingredients in a small saucepan. Cook over medium-high heat until the berries burst and the sauce is glistening, 3 to 5 minutes.

To serve, put 2 crepes on each of 4 plates. Spoon the warm sauce over and garnish each plate with 2 banana spears.

STRAWBERRY SANDWICHES

WHEN I WAS DECIDING ON THE RECIPES FOR THIS COOK-
BOOK, EACH ONE HAD TO PASS THROUGH A THREE-WORD
FILTER: *brilliant, simple cooking. And I think this recipe
truly epitomizes that idea. It's as simple to make as a grilled
cheese sandwich, but the sugar on the outside melts to form a
crème brûlée–like crust while the Brie melts into the fresh
strawberries and jam. This silly delicious combination is one
of the best things I've ever tasted. You saw it here first.*

SERVES 4

½ cup (1 stick) unsalted butter, softened, plus 2 tablespoons for
    browning the sandwiches

8 slices brioche loaf

About ¼ cup granulated sugar

1 jar good-quality strawberry jam

1 pint strawberries, hulled and sliced

6 ounces Brie cheese, thinly sliced, at room temperature

Confectioners' sugar, for dusting

Butter 4 of the brioche slices on both sides. Sprinkle one side with granulated sugar and turn the slices sugared sides down. Spread each slice with jam. Now make a layer of sliced strawberries and cover with slices of cheese. Butter the remaining 4 brioche slices on both sides and sprinkle one side with granulated sugar. Lay the slices on top of the cheese, sugared sides facing up, to make 4 sandwiches. Press down gently.

Heat 1 tablespoon of butter in a cast-iron skillet over medium-low heat. Put 2 of the sandwiches in the pan and cook for 2 to 3 minutes, until the sugar melts, the bread turns golden, and the cheese begins to melt. Turn and cook until the second side is golden and the cheese is bubbly. Take the sandwiches out of the pan and repeat to cook the rest. Dust the sandwiches with confectioners' sugar, cut them in half, and serve warm.

THE ULTIMATE CHOCOLATE MOUSSE

IF YOU'RE A CHOCOLATE LOVER LIKE I AM, HERE'S A SIMPLE WAY TO GET YOUR FIX. *The process is easy. Chocolate melted with butter over a double boiler is enriched with egg yolks, then lightened with whipped egg whites and cream to make a cloudlike consistency: It's amazing and decadent. I like to present mousse in a simple glass for a homemade bistro effect, but the flavor is pure, dense chocolate.*

SERVES 4

6 ounces semisweet chocolate, chopped

3 tablespoons unsalted butter, softened

3 large eggs, separated

½ teaspoon cream of tartar

¼ cup plus 2 tablespoons sugar

½ cup chilled heavy cream

½ teaspoon vanilla extract

Whipped cream and chocolate shavings, for garnish

Bring about 1 inch water just to a simmer in a saucepan; put the chocolate and butter in a heat-proof bowl and set it over the pan, making sure that it doesn't touch water (or use a double boiler). Stir with a wooden spoon until the chocolate is melted and the mixture is smooth. Remove the bowl from the heat and let the mixture cool slightly. Then grab a whisk and beat the egg yolks into the chocolate one at a time, beating until smooth after each addition. Set aside.

In another bowl, beat the egg whites until foamy. Add the cream of tartar and beat until soft peaks form. Gradually beat in ¼ cup of the sugar and continue beating until stiff peaks form.

In a chilled bowl, beat the heavy cream until it begins to thicken up. Add the remaining 2 tablespoons of sugar and the vanilla and continue beating until the cream holds soft peaks.

Now that you've got the elements prepared, put it all together. Stir a spoonful of the egg whites into the chocolate mixture to lighten it, then fold in the rest. Fold in the whipped cream, taking care not to overwork the mousse or it will be heavy. Divide the mousse among 4 glasses. Cover and chill for several hours. Garnish with whipped cream and chocolate shavings before serving.

CHOCOLATE BANANA BREAD

THERE'S AN OLD SAYING IN BAKING THAT THE UGLIEST
FRUIT MAKES THE BEST DESSERTS, *and I completely agree.*
One man's bruised banana is another man's banana bread.
I like to make a loaf of this once a week so I can have a
slice with my coffee in the morning or toast a slice for a
simple dessert.

MAKES 1 LOAF

½ cup (1 stick) unsalted butter, softened, plus more for the pan

2 cups all-purpose flour

¾ cup sugar

¼ cup cocoa powder

1½ teaspoons baking powder

1 teaspoon kosher salt

4 ounces bittersweet chocolate, melted

2 large eggs

3 very ripe bananas

1 teaspoon vanilla extract

Preheat the oven to 350°F. Butter a 9 by 5-inch loaf pan. Mix together the flour, sugar, cocoa powder, baking powder, and salt in a large bowl. In another bowl, cream the butter until lightened, then beat in the chocolate, eggs, bananas, and vanilla. Stir in the dry ingredients just until combined; do not overbeat.

Pour the batter into the loaf pan and bake until a toothpick stuck into the center of the bread comes out almost clean, 50 to 60 minutes. Transfer the pan to a rack and cool for at least 15 minutes before unmolding.

THE ULTIMATE HOT CHOCOLATE

MOST HOT CHOCOLATE RECIPES ACTUALLY CONTAIN VERY LITTLE CHOCOLATE. *They're made instead with cheap cocoa powder, which always tastes flat to me and more like hot chocolate milk than hot chocolate. The ultimate hot chocolate contains layers of flavor: vanilla, coffee beans, and cinnamon. The vanilla acts as a low note and the cinnamon a high note, bracketing the flavor of the chocolate and coffee to give the drink an amazing, well-rounded flavor. And the great thing about this is that everything happens in one pot. When it gets nice and thick, I like to pour it off in espresso cups and then drown a fat marshmallow on top.*

SERVES 4

1 quart milk

2 tablespoons whole coffee beans

1 vanilla bean

1 cinnamon stick

¾ cup sugar

4 ounces bittersweet chocolate, chopped

½ cup cocoa powder

Marshmallows, for serving

Combine the milk, coffee beans, vanilla bean, cinnamon stick, sugar, chocolate, and cocoa powder in a saucepan. Bring it slowly up to a simmer over medium heat, stirring it frequently so that the chocolate doesn't scorch on the bottom of the pan. Strain and serve hot, with marshmallows.

HOMEMADE MARSHMALLOWS (SERVES 4 TO 6)

2 tablespoons powdered gelatin

1 cup cold water

1 cup granulated sugar

1 egg white

1 cup confectioners' sugar, sifted, plus more for dusting (up to an additional 2 cups)

Combine the gelatin and cold water in a medium saucepan. After the gelatin has softened, about 10 minutes, add the granulated sugar and stir together over low heat until the sugar has dissolved, about 8 minutes. Cool the mixture to room temperature.

In a mixer, beat the egg white until it forms stiff peaks. On low, beat in the confectioners' sugar, then slowly pour in the cooled gelatin mixture. Increase the speed to high and beat until the mixture is white, thick, and has doubled in volume.

Line a 9-inch square baking pan with foil, grease it lightly with butter and dust very generously with sifted confectioners' sugar. Pour in the marshmallow mixture and sift more confectioners' sugar over the surface. Let the marshmallows stand at room temperature for at least three hours or overnight to set. The marshmallows will be light and spongy when set.

Loosen the marshmallows from the edges of the pan and invert onto a large cutting board. Peel off the foil and use a large knife to cut the marshmallows into cubes. Dredge each piece in more sifted confectioners' sugar.

CRACKED CHOCOLATE EARTH

THIS RECIPE GETS ITS NAME FROM THE WAY THE CAKE
LOOKS WHEN IT FALLS AFTER IT COMES OUT OF THE OVEN.
*It's unavoidable and beautiful at the same time. The recipe
uses only four ingredients: chocolate, butter, eggs, and sugar.
To smell this cake baking is like chocolate aromatherapy.*

SERVES 8

1 cup (2 sticks) unsalted butter, cut up, plus more for the pan
1 pound bittersweet chocolate, chopped into small pieces
9 large eggs, separated
3/4 cup granulated sugar
Confectioners' sugar, for dusting

Preheat the oven to 350°F. Butter a 9-inch springform pan.

Put the chocolate and butter into the top of a double boiler (or in a heat-proof bowl) and heat over (but not touching) about 1 inch of simmering water until melted. Meanwhile, whisk the egg yolks with the sugar in a mixing bowl until light yellow in color. Whisk a little of the warm chocolate mixture into the egg-yolk mixture to temper the eggs—this will keep the eggs from scrambling from the heat of the chocolate—then whisk in the rest of the chocolate mixture.

Beat the egg whites in a mixing bowl until stiff peaks form, and fold into the chocolate mixture. Pour into the prepared pan and bake until the cake is set, the top starts to crack, and a toothpick inserted into the cake comes out with moist crumbs clinging to it, 20 to 25 minutes. Let the cake stand for 10 minutes, then release the sides of the pan. Serve at room temperature, dusted with confectioners' sugar.

VANILLA POTS DE CRÈME

IF YOU LOVE CRÈME BRÛLÉE BUT THE IDEA OF LIGHTING UP A PROPANE TORCH IN YOUR KITCHEN MAKES YOU A LITTLE NERVOUS, THEN THIS IS THE WAY TO GO. *It's a delicious vanilla custard that you can make a day ahead of time and round off with a dessert wine and amaretti cookies.*

SERVES 6

1½ cups milk

1½ cups heavy cream

5 large egg yolks

½ cup sugar

1 teaspoon vanilla extract

Amaretti cookies, for serving

Preheat the oven to 325°F and bring a saucepan of water to a boil for a water bath.

Pour the milk and cream into a saucepan and place over medium-low heat. Bring just to a simmer, then remove from the heat.

In a large bowl, whisk together the egg yolks and sugar until the sugar starts to dissolve and the yolks turn light yellow, about 3 minutes. Gradually whisk in the hot cream mixture, a thin stream at first so as not to cook the yolks, and then more quickly. Stir in the vanilla.

Pour the custard mixture into six 8-ounce ramekins or cappuccino cups and cover each with a square of foil to keep a crust from forming. Place the ramekins into a large, shallow baking pan and set the pan on the oven rack. Pour ½ inch of boiling water into the baking pan for the water bath. Carefully slide the rack into place and bake for about 45 minutes, until the custard is set but the center still jiggles slightly. Remove the pan from the oven and let the ramekins cool in the water for 10 minutes. Then pop them in the fridge to chill for at least 2 hours. Serve with cookies.

ICE CREAM "BOULDERS"

THIS IS A KID-FRIENDLY DESSERT THAT WILL BE A BIG HIT AT THE NEXT BIRTHDAY PARTY. *It's simply big, fat scoops of ice cream rolled in whatever—ground Oreos, M&M's, toffee bars, you name it—and refrozen. It's fast because the boulders are constructed entirely of store-bought ingredients. There's a recipe for an absolutely delicious caramel sauce, too, but if you're short on time, feel free to substitute any gooey ice-cream topping that looks good at the store: strawberry sauce, chocolate sauce, butterscotch—it all works. This is my son's favorite and the recipe is his idea.*

SERVES 6 TO 8

½ pound chocolate sandwich cookies, such as Oreos

½ pound toffee bars

½ pound M&M's

½ pound Reese's Pieces

½ gallon good-quality vanilla ice cream

CARAMEL SAUCE

¾ cup sugar

4 tablespoons (½ stick) unsalted butter, cut into pieces

¾ cup heavy cream

Put the cookies, toffee bars, M&M's, and Reese's Pieces in separate resealable bags and crush each with a rolling pin; spread each on a separate plate. Line a baking sheet with parchment or wax paper. Using a large ice-cream scoop, scoop out a big, round "boulder" of ice cream and use two forks to roll it in one or more of the crushed toppings to cover. Using the forks, carefully transfer the "boulder" to the prepared baking sheet. Repeat to make as many "boulders" as you wish. Cover the baking sheet with plastic wrap and put it in the freezer while you make the sauce.

Combine the sugar and ¼ cup of water in a heavy-bottomed saucepan over medium heat. Give it a stir. Bring to a boil, reduce the heat, and let it simmer, without stirring, until the syrup cooks down to a caramel, 10 to 15 minutes. As the sugar caramelizes, swirl the pan for even color. Remove from the heat. Carefully add the butter (stand back: the sugar will bubble like crazy). Then, wearing an oven mitt to protect your hand, stir. Slowly pour in the cream and stir until smooth. Serve the "boulders" with the caramel sauce.

SANGRIA GRANITA WITH COLD SPIKED FRUIT

THIS RECIPE WAS A HUGE HIT WHEN WE TESTED IT. *It seemed a little complicated in theory but once we put it together it was nothing more than a flavored slushy. The spiced sangria gets poured into a lasagna pan and frozen overnight and the fresh fruit, tossed with Cointreau and sugar, gets frozen as well.*

For a sleek presentation I serve this in a glass. The frozen fruit goes in the bottom and acts like ice cubes to keep the granita colder longer. On a summer day, there's nothing more refreshing.

SERVES 6 TO 8

SANGRIA GRANITA

1 bottle (750 ml) red wine

½ cup sugar

½ cup Cointreau

4 whole cloves

1 cinnamon stick

½ lemon, seeded

½ orange, seeded

COLD SPIKED FRUIT

2 peaches, pitted and quartered but not peeled

2 cups red or green grapes, halved

1 pint strawberries, hulled and halved

½ cup Cointreau

2 tablespoons sugar

Fresh mint, for garnish

For the granita, combine the wine, sugar, Cointreau, and spices in a large saucepan. Squeeze the juice from the lemon and orange halves; add the juice to the saucepan and throw in the squeezed halves, too. Warm for about 5 minutes over medium heat, stirring to dissolve the sugar. Strain into a bowl and put the mixture in the fridge or over an ice bath to chill.

Pour the chilled mixture into a shallow baking pan and freeze for at least 1 hour or overnight, until the mixture is frozen. Using a fork or a couple of chopsticks, break up all the ice crystals on the bottom and sides of the pan. (This aerates the mixture so that the finished granita will melt in your mouth.) Freeze for 3 to 4 more hours, until the mixture is frozen but still granular.

Meanwhile, combine the peaches, grapes, and strawberries in a bowl, add the Cointreau and sugar, and toss. Cover and put the bowl in the freezer for a couple of hours; the fruit will absorb the sugar and liqueur while it freezes. Serve the frozen fruit with the granita and garnish with mint.

PEACH CARDINAL

WHEN PEACHES ARE SO JUICY THAT THE JUICE RUNS DOWN TO YOUR ELBOWS WHEN YOU BITE INTO THEM, IT'S THE PERFECT TIME OF YEAR TO MAKE THIS DESSERT.

———————

SERVES 4

2 pints fresh raspberries

¼ cup fresh orange juice

1 tablespoon sugar, plus extra for sprinkling

2 ripe peaches

1 lemon

6 tablespoons unsalted butter, softened

2 brioche slices, cut ¼ inch thick

Combine the raspberries, orange juice, and 1 tablespoon of sugar in a saucepan and cook over medium-high heat until the raspberries turn to mush, about 5 minutes. Strain out the seeds and throw the bowl in the fridge to chill.

Bring a saucepan of water to a boil and fill a bowl with ice water. Put the peaches in a heat-proof bowl and pour over the hot water to cover; let stand for about 3 minutes. Then take the peaches out of the hot water with a slotted spoon and put them in the ice water; peel off the skins with a small paring knife. Cut the peaches in half and remove the pits. Squeeze lemon juice over the peaches to keep them from discoloring.

Preheat the oven to 350°F. Butter both sides of the brioche slices and sprinkle with sugar on both sides. Cut each on a diagonal into 2 triangles. Fit the triangles into a muffin tin to give them a rounded shape. Put the muffin tin in the oven and toast until the bread is crispy and browned, about 10 minutes.

To serve, spoon some of the chilled raspberry sauce into 4 small bowls. Add the peach halves and garnish the bowls with the warm brioche wedges.

ALMOND SEMIFREDDO WITH DRIED FRUIT AND SPICED HONEY

IF YOU'VE NEVER MADE SEMIFREDDO BEFORE, TRY IT—*it's sensational. It's cold, creamy, and frozen like ice cream but light as air. You freeze it in a loaf pan and it's perfect for dinner parties. Impressive and outrageous, it's homemade ice cream without the machine.*

SERVES 8

2½ cups milk

6 large egg yolks

⅔ cup sugar

1 teaspoon vanilla extract

1 tablespoon amaretto liqueur

½ cup chopped almonds

1½ cups heavy cream

SPICED HONEY

6 figs, fresh or dried, cut into quarters

6 dates, pitted and chopped

½ cup honey

Juice of 1 lemon

1 cinnamon stick

Pour the milk into a saucepan and bring just to a boil over medium-high heat.

In a large bowl, whisk together the egg yolks and sugar until the sugar starts to dissolve and the yolks turn light yellow, about 3 minutes. Gradually whisk in the hot milk, adding it in a thin stream at first so as not to cook the yolks, and then more quickly. Return the mixture to the saucepan and cook over low heat without boiling, until the mixture thickly coats the back of a spoon, 4 to 5 minutes. Remove the custard from the heat and stir in the vanilla and amaretto. Refrigerate until cool (or chill in a water bath).

Preheat the oven to 350°F. Spread the almonds on a baking sheet and toast until golden and fragrant, 7 to 10 minutes.

When the custard is cold, whip the cream to stiff peaks and fold into the custard along with the toasted almonds. Scrape the mixture into a 9 by 5-inch loaf pan, cover, and freeze.

Meanwhile, put the figs, dates, honey, ¼ cup of water, lemon juice, and cinnamon stick in a small saucepan and bring to a simmer over medium heat. Cook for about 10 minutes, or until the fruit is soft. Let cool slightly, then discard the cinnamon stick.

To serve, dip the bottom of the loaf pan in a bowl of hot water for 5 seconds. Put a platter on top and then invert quickly; lift off the loaf pan. Cut the semifreddo into slices and put the slices on plates. Spoon some of the spiced honey over each slice.

ACKNOWLEDGMENTS: HERE'S TO ALL MY FRIENDS

FOR THEIR HELP WITH THE BOOK:

Petrina Tinslay, Stephanie Lyness, Ruba Abu-Nimah, Henry Leutwyler, Chris Berry, Amy McCafferty; everyone at Clarkson Potter: including my editor, Pam Krauss, Jane Treuhaft, Marysarah Quinn, Amy Boorstein, Joan Denman, Tammy Blake, and Amy Corley; Lisa Hecht, and Eileen Connors.

TO MY FOOD NETWORK FAMILY:

Mark Dissin, Emily Reiger, Jimmy Zankel, Bob Tuschman, Brooke Johnson, Allison Page, everyone in the culinary department, Robert Bleifer, Jay Brooks, Wendy Waxman, and all of my colleagues: Bobby, Paula, Rachael, Giada, Emeril, Dave, George, The Hearty Boys, Michael, Cat, Mario, Morimoto, Alton, et al.

TO MY BRILLIANT GROUP OF FRIENDS:

The Lekometros Family, the Wynter-Stoner Family, Max MacKenzie, Jillian Matlock, The Rose Family, The DeBartolo Family, Maxine Ganer, Andrei Petrov & Emma, Rick Eisenberg, Marisa Polvino, Benny Rietveld, Art Smith & Linda Novick O'Keefe at Common Threads, Govind Armstrong, Todd English, Frankie DeCarlo, Jen Andrews, Jerry Penacoli, Ryan Seacrest, The Old School Cargo Magazine Crew: Lance Ford, Ariel Foxman & Matt Trainor, Greg DiStefano, Rocco DiSpirito, Marcus Samuelsson, Tony Sepulveda, Drew Nieporent, Lee Schrager, Caryl Chinn, Riad Nasr and everyone at Balthazar, John Orgera, and the DiPalo Family.

TO MY BUSINESS PARTNERS:

My agents at the William Morris Agency: Jeff Googel, Jason Hodes, Jon Rosen; Mikasa & Arc International; Applebee's; WOR Radio; Braun; James Luria and everyone at AOL; The Marshall Fields/Macy's Culinary Council, especially Warren Wolfe & Kelly Lainsbury; Andy Cohan & everyone at Magna Global; my partners at Bar Florence, Chris Heyman & Josh Woodward; Reid Strathearn at Meridian Entertainment; John Wyatt & everyone at Tentation, Potel & Chabot; Johnson & Wales University; Brian Maynard & KitchenAid.

TO THE FAMILY, SOME RELATED & SOME UNRELATED:

My son, Miles, Mom & John, Dad & Jan, Michael, Ryan, Uncle Worm & Jenna, Ruth Rojas, Kristi, Alycia, Laura Hiser, Anthony Hoy Fong, The Clark/ Moss/Cohen/Krahl families in Marin, and especially my girl-friend Tolan Clark & our dog Jake.

LASTLY, JAKE "BACON" FLORENCE WOULD LIKE TO THANK:

Fresh Direct for all of the delicious bacon & always being on time, Café Habana for the tasty treats, Cathy from California (you know who you are), my special brother Eddie, Chavez Emilio Delgado from Brooklyn, Viking for the worlds best refrigerator and ice maker (I love ice), Bailey, my cousin Susie, Chelsea Market for allowing me to sneak in to the Food Network when my Dad is shooting his show, Buckwheat, DiPalo's Dairy for the best prosciutto in the world, Jeffrey the crazy butcher at the Essex Street Market, Schiller's Liquor Bar for delicious delivery two nights a week, the lady with the braid, and Charleston Magazine for putting me on the cover. In closing, he would like to leave you with some words of wisdom: "Why's bacon got to be so delicious?"

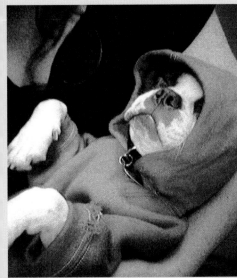  

INDEX

CONVERSION CHART

EQUIVALENT IMPERIAL AND METRIC MEASUREMENTS

American cooks use standard containers, the 8-ounce cup and a tablespoon that takes exactly 16 level fillings to fill that cup level. Measuring by cup makes it very difficult to give weight equivalents, as a cup of densely packed butter will weigh considerably more than a cup of flour. The easiest way therefore to deal with cup measurements in recipes is to take the amount by volume rather than by weight. Thus the equation reads:

1 cup = 240 ml = 8 fl. oz.   ½ cup = 120 ml = 4 fl. oz.

In the States, butter is often measured in sticks. One stick is the equivalent of 8 tablespoons. One tablespoon of butter is therefore equivalent to ½ ounce/15 grams.

LIQUID MEASURES

Fluid Ounces	U.S.	Imperial	Milliliters
⅛	1 teaspoon	1 teaspoon	5
¼	2 teaspoons	1 dessertspoon	10
½	1 tablespoon	1 tablespoon	14
1	2 tablespoons	2 tablespoons	28
2	¼ cup	4 tablespoons	56
4	½ cup		120
5		¼ pint or 1 gill	140
6	¾ cup		170
8	1 cup		240
9			250, ¼ liter
10	1¼ cups	½ pint	280
12	1½ cups		340
15		¾ pint	420
16	2 cups		450
18	2¼ cups		500, ½ liter
20	2½ cups	1 pint	560
24	3 cups		675
25		1¼ pints	700
27	3½ cups		750
30	3¾ cups	1½ pints	840
32	4 cups or 1 quart		900
35		1¾ pints	980
36	4½ cups		1000, 1 liter
40	5 cups	2 pints or 1 quart	1120

SOLID MEASURES

U.S. AND IMPERIAL MEASURES		METRIC MEASURES	
Ounces	Pounds	Grams	Kilos
1		28	
2		56	
3½		100	
4	¼	112	
5		140	
6		168	
8	½	225	
9		250	¼
12	¾	340	
16	1	450	
18		500	½
20	1¼	560	
24	1½	675	
27		750	¾
28	1¾	780	
32	2	900	
36	2¼	1000	1
40	2½	1100	
48	3	1350	
54		1500	1½

OVEN TEMPERATURE EQUIVALENTS

Fahrenheit	Celsius	Gas Mark	Description
225	110	¼	Cool
250	130	½	
275	140	1	Very Slow
300	150	2	
325	170	3	Slow
350	180	4	Moderate
375	190	5	
400	200	6	Moderately Hot
425	220	7	Fairly Hot
450	230	8	Hot
475	240	9	Very Hot
500	250	10	Extremely Hot

Any broiling recipes can be used with the grill of the oven, but beware of high-temperature grills.

EQUIVALENTS FOR INGREDIENTS

all-purpose flour—plain flour
baking sheet—oven tray
buttermilk—ordinary milk
cheesecloth—muslin
coarse salt—kitchen salt
cornstarch—cornflour
eggplant—aubergine

granulated sugar—castor sugar
half and half—12% fat milk
heavy cream—double cream
light cream—single cream
lima beans—broad beans
parchment paper—greaseproof paper
plastic wrap—cling film

scallion—spring onion
shortening—white fat
unbleached flour—strong, white flour
vanilla bean—vanilla pod
zest—rind
zucchini—courgettes or marrow